ping

ping

how to tap into the
power of traditional
and social media
to massively improve
your profile and profits

alan stevens

bookshaker

First Published in Great Britain 2009
www.BookShaker.com

To my father, Steve, who died almost
50 years ago, but taught me the principles
that I still live by today. Thanks Dad.

To Blake Snyder, genius scriptwriter,
author of one of the greatest books about
cinema (Save the Cat), and a brief
but dear friend. Much missed.

Praise

"The notion of integrating PR – with social media and marketing - is more prevalent now than ever. A disconnect between departments or functions can spell disaster for companies, and Alan understands that perfectly. Alan provides some concrete examples of companies that are doing it well and some guideposts for those looking to embark upon the process."

Scott Monty, Digital & Multimedia Communications Manager, Ford Motor Company

"I love this book, and I'll be recommending it to all my clients! Alan clearly knows what he's talking about; he tells the behind-the-scenes truth about what journalists want, and he offers practical, common-sense tips, principles and case studies that any business anywhere in the world is sure to benefit from."

Kay Ross, a Hong Kong-based marketing consultant/coach, editor and former journalist at the South China Morning Post, www.kayross.com

"It's brilliant! Page after page packed with useful information on how to promote your business effectively. it will become a must-have for anybody looking to get the best out of the media for their business."

Carole Clayton, Owner, The Rural Meeting Place www.theruralmeetingplace.com

"Alan gets it. The book does a great job of demonstrating how to evolve traditional PR and marketing strategies to comply with the digital world."

Amy Martin, Director, Digital Royalty, Phoenix Arizona, www.thedigitalroyalty.com

"Ping is a book any business; whether small or large; or any person will find useful. Whether you are savvy with social media or just starting out; the case studies and features in the book will be useful and of value to any reader."

Cole Imperi, Creative Director, Doth Brands, www.coleimperi.com

"Alan demystifies and simplifies the whole industry of public relations and social media with a simple step by step process."

Fred Shadian, Nutritional Microscopist, www.fredshadian.com

"This is a 'must have' guide and reference book for those companies looking for practical advice on an integrated PR approach. An enjoyable read and highly recommended."

Julia Payne Co-Founder Incisive Edge, www.incisive-edge.com

"This is an enjoyable and easy to read, concise and comprehensive, strategic and simple, plus timeless and up to the minute guide for building your brand and its relationships with clients and broader community through all the media. Decades of experience in a potent package."

**Robin Wheeler,
Transformation Specialist and Author of the INSIGHTS series of books, www.bentrepreneuring.com**

"Many organisations want to build visibility for their business with the media, and increasingly are turning to social media from Twitter to YouTube, from blogs to Facebook to bring their message to potential customers and stakeholders. These are free or low cost to implement (though they do require investment of time to get real benefit from these platforms). However with this mad dash for the mouse, many business owners are forgetting the benefit of integrating their online communications with their overall communications plan. Media Coach and UK communications expert, Alan Stevens, provides guidance in his new book in how to ensure your PR and communications plan incorporates traditional and new media. It's accessible and practical, so if you are looking for guidance in how to create a comprehensive PR campaign, make sure you read and put into practice Alan's advice."

Krishna De, CEO of Biz Growth Media, a digital marketing and social media agency, www.bizgrowthnews.com

"It's great. I like the easy bite-sized pieces. The advice on traditional media is very useful - many people are daunted by the prospect of contacting journalists, etc, so insider tips on how to approach print, TV and radio coverage are invaluable. The social media advice is also very helpful- it's easy to get submerged by Twitter/Facebook etc. and these guidelines offer a sensible, and level-headed, way of looking at it. With all the buzz about social and viral marketing at the moment, it's sometimes difficult to know where to turn!"

Carolyn Bennett, Marketing Director, Chalets Direct www.chaletsdirect.com

"I Really liked this book; thorough, direct and very little fat on the bone. And very useful indeed. As I intimated on the phone, it's discovering what you didn't know that's often key. And your advice certainly compelled me, as a result, to read on and pick up some pretty invaluable tips and tricks."

Jeremy Kay, Director, Nowhouse www.nowhouse.tv

"Alan is a master at simplifying the complicated for what seems daunting to many of us. The book is easy to understand and the various tasks interesting and doable."

Susan Luke, International Speaker and Corporate Mythologist, www.susanluke.com

"This is an excellent book both as a reference guide and also real life examples to illustrate the beneficial outcomes. Wish it had been available when I started my business two years' ago - I would say that it is an essential read for anyone starting up a business who wants to get noticed and formulate an integrated media strategy."

Yvonne Goodwin, Managing Director, Yvonne Goodwin Wealth Management, www.yvonnegoodwin.co.uk

"I love it! For me it took away the need to go on all those 'teach yourself PR' courses with the added bonus of learning about applying the principles to new social media."

Amanda Brown, PR and Communications Director, First Direct, www.firstdirect.com

Acknowledgements

My thanks, as ever, to my wife and Business Manager, Heather Waring, without whom this book would have remained an idea, albeit a good one!

Thanks also to my publishers, Debbie Jenkins and Joe Gregory at Bookshaker, who continue to have faith in my ability to turn out words to a deadline.

Finally, thanks to the unsung heroes of the media; the writers of social networking systems, the drivers of cars to the studios and the coffee makers and biscuit providers. We couldn't do it without you. Thanks.

Contents

Foreword

In the late 18th Century, Georgiana Cavendish, Duchess of Devonshire, was the mistress of Charles James Fox, a prominent politician and staunch opponent of the monarch, George III.

She decided to throw all her efforts into raising his profile. Her methods included press relations, lobbying and, with her friends, celebrity campaigning. Largely as a result of her campaign, Fox won the parliamentary seat of Westminster by a narrow margin, though legal challenges (largely orchestrated by the King and William Pitt, the Prime Minister) held up the final declaration of the result for over a year. The first example of public relations (PR) in practice.

These days, the relationship between client and PR agency is more chaste.

Over 200 years later, Georgiana's descendents, including Diana, Princess of Wales, and Sarah, Duchess of York, used public relations techniques extensively to make sure that their points of view were communicated to and understood by as wide an audience as possible. The same practice is followed by all figures in public life, as well as by every business, large or small.

Lately, we have seen the rise of web-based PR, using a variety of sites and applications. But the principles remain the same.

PR is about managing the flow of information between an organisation (and I use the term to include celebrities) and the public. That's all there is to it. These days, the flow is not one-way. The change that is happening now is particularly around the flow of information from the public – you and me - back to an organisation. Some organisations are handling the change better than others.

So this book is not really about new things. It's about long-recognised principles applied with old and new tools. I hope that Georgiana and Charles would be pleased with it.

Alan Stevens
London, 2009

Introduction

This book shows you how you can promote your business, and raise your profile, at very little cost, to an audience larger than you ever thought possible. The result? More clients.

I have been in the media for over 25 years, as an expert interviewee, presenter, producer and journalist. I have been on both sides of the camera and microphone. I know what works.

You can promote your business when times are tough, when times are good, at any time at all. It doesn't matter a bit. These techniques work anywhere, anytime. Don't worry about journalists learning the plan. They know the rules too, and are happy to play along. Always remember, journalists are your friends. They are just like pets. If you are nice to them, feed them, make their lives easier by making sure they have what they need, they will repay you with loyalty, coming back over and over again.

I intend to show you how to make journalists happy, and in turn benefit from masses of publicity (though the journalist will call it objective reporting).

I have never met a journalist who wasn't delighted when someone gave them a story to appeal to their audience.

A word of warning: Never, ever, thank a journalist for giving you publicity. By all means praise their journalistic skills and balanced view. If they ever think that they are acting as your unpaid publicist, they can turn nasty.

The rules of the PR game are here in this book. Read them carefully and heed them well. If you understand and apply them, your business will soar. None of the rules in here is difficult to learn or costly to implement. Apply them; if not, you have only yourself to blame.

OK, pep talk over. Let's get started.

What is Integrated PR?

This book is not about social media (MySpace, LinkedIn, Twitter), nor about traditional media (TV, radio and print). It's about both. The important thing (in my opinion) is to use as many different channels as possible to deliver your message. That's not to say that just using radio advertising, or a campaign on Twitter, is a bad thing. My contention is that you should use as many options as you can in a single campaign.

I define integrated PR as A PR campaign which delivers a single core message, using both traditional and social media.

First, you need a message. The art of good PR is to be able to convey the right one, in the right way, at the right time, to the right audience. The essence of a message is always the precise detail we wish to impart.

So, how do you create this core message for your integrated PR campaign?

Here is a checklist of the most important elements:

1) Identify The Single Most Important Idea

People remember very little of what they see or hear. The most effective PR campaigns focus on the most important message that you wish to communicate, since that's what you want people to remember.

If you have several messages you want to deliver, save the less important ones for another time. One message that is remembered by your potential clients is worth dozens of half-remembered ones.

2) Keep It Simple

Don't use jargon, or industry-specific terms. It's impossible to over-simplify a message, but easy to over-complicate one.

3) Make It Memorable

We are besieged with messages every day, through radio and TV, adverts, conversations and the like. Your job, when delivering your message on the media, is to make it something that people will remember. Think of words and phrases that are a little unusual, or conjure up an image. If your message is seen as a picture, even if you are on the radio, it will be much more memorable.

4) Make It Relevant

Put yourself in the shoes of your potential audience and think what they will find engaging. All you have to do then is to deliver what they want to see or hear.

5) Ask Yourself "So What?"

Imagine yourself hearing your own core message. If your immediate reaction is "so what?" the message doesn't work. You need to be able to capture the value to your audience in whatever you say.

7) Be Sincere

If you want people to believe you, you have to be sincere. You have to really believe what you are saying. That is why it is very important for you, as a company spokesperson, to be involved in drafting the core message. It will be very difficult for you to recite words given to you by a PR person if you are not fully confident that they represent your opinion.

In summary then, your core message needs to be simple, relevant, memorable, beneficial and, of course, true. How hard is that?

Free Publicity – What It Is, And How To Get It

There's no such thing as a free lunch, they say. Actually, they are wrong. With my journalist badge on, I have had plenty of free lunches, though a sausage on a stick, a curled up tuna sandwich and a glass of lukewarm chardonnay barely merit the term. Journalists are invited to no end of events, including (but not limited to) press conferences, product launches, restaurant openings, boat trips and even the occasional night club. Very few of them result in a good story about the company who invited them along. On most occasions, the assembled hacks will talk amongst themselves about every topic under the sun, other than the pretext on which they were invited. Later on, they will dig the press release out of the press pack, re-word a few of the sentences, add a little spin of their own in a punning headline, and hand it to their sub-editor. This is not the way to get free publicity.

Let's look at things another way. Despite the ubiquity of the Internet, there are more print publications than ever before. Every specialist niche has its own stable of magazines and newspapers. There are tens of thousands of journalists, each looking for something to write about. You can help them, simply by being visible and being willing to put yourself out, just a little, when they ask you for a quote or an interview. It is very unlikely that you will be interrogated, or find yourself on the wrong end of a series of tough questions. The only rule of the game, nearly all the time, is this:

> **The reporter wants you to tell your story in simple terms that capture the interest of their audience.**

That's it. If you remember nothing else about media relations, carry that phrase in your head for the rest of your life. It will get you on air, and ensure that you are invited back time and time again.

Very few people appear in the media by accident. Reporters don't have time to go looking for sources. Your job is to get to know people in the media (without becoming a pest), and to provide them with the help they need to complete their story, so that they can get a pat on the head from their editor and go home happy.

That's what the rest of this book is about. It will help you start on your path to becoming the Go to person for your topic. Heeding the advice in here is a start.

Using The Media

When I say using, I don't mean abusing. Your relationship with reporters needs to be one of mutual respect and mutual benefit. That becomes very easy as soon as you learn to think like a journalist.

With all types of communication, the key is to be able to understand the person that you are talking to, discover what they want, and give it to them. Journalists are regarded by many people with suspicion, because they are seen as interrogators who will try to make you reveal information. While it is true that there are a few journalists who adopt this adversarial approach (you know who I mean), most journalists are just like you and me. They have a job to do, which is to fill a few column inches in a newspaper, a 30-second report on the lunchtime news bulletin, or a five-second sound bite for the TV *News at Ten.*

They are often under pressure, harassed and desperate to finish a job almost before it is started.

The main motivation of a reporter is to complete the task given them by their editor, as quickly and efficiently as possible. If you can help them to do this, you will find that the interaction will go well, and you will become a trusted contact that they will return to again and again for expert comment.

When you are being interviewed, your aim is to get your message across as succinctly as possible. The aim of the interviewer is to find out what you know, and encourage you to explain it as clearly as possible. There is a common interest here. Rather than being wary of journalists, you should see them as willing partners in the business of message delivery. Almost everyone you meet in the media will be friendly and helpful, if you are friendly and helpful to them. If you approach an interview with mistrust, trying to guard your secrets, not only will you not enjoy the experience, but you will make future interviews more difficult.

I'm not suggesting that you should invite every journalist you meet round for dinner. However, treating them with courtesy, respect and general friendliness will pay dividends, and will guarantee that they are unlikely to be combative.

If and when you do come up against an interviewer who spurns your chummy approach, there are other techniques you will need to use; we'll learn about those later in this book.

A journalist will always be thinking, "what will interest my audience?"

You need to be thinking along the same lines.

You need to find out as much as possible about their audience in advance of the interviews and tailor your responses accordingly.

For example, let's say you are an IT company launching a new piece of software that makes it easier for small companies to complete their tax returns. You need to find the right moment and the right trigger to make the journalist (on behalf of their audience) very keen to talk to you. So you put yourself in the position of a small business owner, working all hours, faced with the prospect of either a large accountant's bill, or hours slaving over a spreadsheet and a self-assessment manual.

The best time to talk about the software is? NOT two weeks before the tax returns are due in. Your audience will be far too busy to take any notice of stories in the press. The best time is just after returns have been submitted, when you can use contrasting case studies of those people who used your software, and those who didn't.

Do you need a news hook? Try *Companies in <your locality here> save a fortune at tax time*. It sounds a bit like an advertisement (hooray!), but it really is a story, since it has local interest, topicality and a human angle. The fact that your company and its products get mentioned is just a bonus.

When A Reporter Calls

In all your dealings with the media, you need to be media-ready. You will probably experience a variety of emotions when a call arrives from a journalist; panic, flattery, excitement or nervousness (probably a combination of all of these). If you respond immediately, any of these emotions will affect your response, causing you to say something that you may later regret.

When a reporter calls, you need to buy some time to gather your thoughts. It really doesn't matter what excuse you use. You could say that you have a phone call on another line, that you have an urgent appointment, or even that you have to answer a call of nature. The reporter may object briefly, but they understand the rules of the game as well as you do.

Before you put down the phone, there is some vital information that you must acquire. You need to know the **name** of the journalist, **where** they are from, the **subject** of the enquiry, and their **contact details**.

Don't ask what their deadline is, since the answer will almost always be five minutes ago.

Note down the details carefully, thank them for their call, and promise to call them back within a few minutes. If you receive calls from the press regularly, it will pay to have a standard form to hand, which you keep by your phone (don't forget to have a form and pen with you at all times, since journalists will also have your mobile phone number).

Now, you have six or seven minutes to prepare yourself.

If you know your stuff, write down the key message you want to deliver. If you aren't quite sure, phone a friend who is better informed. Give some thought to any tricky questions that may be asked, and consider how you will respond. Set yourself a few targets, such as mentioning your web site three times. After about 10 minutes, call them back. Don't be late.

Stunning Facts

Reporters are looking for much more than facts. They are looking for a story. The way in which you present facts can make the difference between being reported and being ignored.

If you are speaking on behalf of an aircraft manufacturer, you may well have a mass of facts about a new aircraft. Some of them may be quite astonishing (to you, at least), and you decide, correctly, to include them during your interview. Let's say that the wingspan of your new passenger plane is the largest of any commercial airliner, stretching to just over 90 metres.

You say to the interviewer, "Our new airliner is enormous, with a wingspan of 91.5 metres". While true, that fact won't resonate with the audience, since most of them can't visualise what it means.

However, if you say, "The wings on our airliner are so large, they would stretch from one penalty spot to the other on a football pitch".

Now you've impressed the audience, and they are imagining being at their local football ground and seeing your plane covering most of the playing area.

You should always try to link your facts to examples that will make them come alive. Once you have come up with a stunning fact, use it over and over again in interviews and publicity material, so that people will remember it.

You can always tell when a stunning fact has hit home. You will find it referred to in stories on air, in newspapers, and on the internet. If you really hit the jackpot, you may even find it quoted back to you in conversation, although, alas, people probably won't know who coined the phrase.

7 Ways to Hit the Target With Your Press Release

Press releases are vital tools in the PR armoury.

Here are seven ways to avoid firing blanks

1. Have an obvious angle or hook
Journalists need to have an angle for every story. If your press release doesn't have one in the first few words, it will end up in the bin.

2. Deliver a new story
There must be an element of news. If the story has been covered before, or happened a long time ago, there won't be any journalistic interest

3. Make your headline clear
Does your headline pass the poster test? Trying to be too clever, with puns or double meanings, can backfire.

4. Make the story short and clear
If the story is not obvious, the release is not doing its job.

5. Include quotes
These are vital to give real interest to a story.

6. Include controversy if you can
Don't be boring - would you read a boring article?

7. Give all your contact details
Better make sure you take your computer to bed if you only give your email address.

Are You One Of Them, Or One Of Us?

Many clients that I work with have highly-paid positions in large organisations. That's why they are asked to appear on TV and radio. An issue they sometimes struggle with is how to relate to the day-to-day problems faced by their customers. If you have people to drive you around, organise your day, and follow your orders, you may be perceived as one of them.

Phrases such as fat cat may be used by your opponents to further this perception. If you find yourself thus categorised, how can you change people's views?

Some bosses seem to be able to do this effortlessly. Richard Branson represents the Virgin brand often. It's not natural, it's something he's learnt. In fact, he is very nervous before any media interviews, but knows that he has to appear. He has nurtured his common touch by visiting his businesses regularly, and talking to staff and customers. A number of CEOs behave in a similar way, but not nearly enough.

It is essential you understand, and can relate to, the issues that face your audience. If you don't understand how they feel, you will come across as aloof and distant. Make the point that you are a user of your own services (you are, aren't you?), or that you regularly visit the front line.

Don't pretend to be what you're not. William Hague, great speaker that he is, took a long time to live down the image of wearing a baseball cap to the Notting Hill Carnival, trying to be a regular guy. What you must do is understand and empathise with your audience. They will love you for it.

Monitor Your Media Coverage

Consistency is very important when it comes to media relations. If you have more than one media spokesperson, they need to deliver a similar message. Even if only one person speaks to reporters, they need to know what they said to a reporter in a previous interview, however long ago. That's where media monitoring comes in.

After every media interview or contact, you should record your impressions. Note the date, time and topic, as well as your recollection of what was said. If it is a print interview, keep the clipping. You may also be able to get hold of a copy of a radio or TV interview, so keep that on file too. It takes only a few minutes each time, and you will find that it becomes an invaluable resource. I'm constantly amazed by the small number of companies that do monitor their media coverage. Oddly enough, the ones that do this seem to be more successful, and have a better image.

You can employ agencies to monitor your media coverage, and most also offer an evaluation service. Not all media bureaux handle both print and broadcast, so you may have to shop around, or employ two companies. You may find it possible to maintain records yourself (assuming you don't get much coverage). So if you need an agency, it's a sign of success or notoriety - I assume you'll know which.

When should you start monitoring? Next time you speak to a reporter (even if it doesn't lead to an interview). In the years to come, you'll be glad you kept records.

News Never Sleeps

Today, more than at any time in history, news is a 24-hour rolling stream. It never stops. This has both advantages and disadvantages. News media are engaged in constant competition to break stories, provide new angles, and secure the services of the best analysts and pundits to comment on and analyse stories.

If you appear on TV, you may find your remarks repeated on radio, quoted in newspapers, and appearing on websites. In short, there is no hiding place. Exclusivity, if it exists at all, is measured in seconds rather than minutes or hours. Once a story has broken, somewhere, you become fair game for reporters.

How do you cope? Well, luckily, there are some things you can do to relieve the stress. Google Alerts are email updates of the latest mentions of any word or phrase that you specify. They can be sent to you daily, weekly or as they appear. You should definitely have Google alerts set up permanently for your name and your organisation name. If a crisis occurs, set up new alerts that relate to it. Monitor them constantly so that you will be ready to respond.

The other important thing is to have a 24-hour news contact. That doesn't have to be you, but it must be a real person, with a number that is made known through your press office, or (very importantly) on the press area of your website. You do have a press area, don't you? Well, I'll tell you more about setting one up soon.

7 Ways To Get International Publicity

Want to be known worldwide? Here are some tips.

1. Learn about the international media
Read websites, journals and listen to web radio. Show that you know something about a media outlet when you talk to them.

2. Make an approach
Talk to radio and TV station editors. Make a connection between their programming and your expertise. Offer to be interviewed at any time, at very short notice.

3. Sell a story, not information
Human interest works well. So does conflict. These things are of interest everywhere in the world. The more unusual, the better

4. Make a commitment to the media
Decide what you want to achieve - a radio interview on BBC World for example. Put a timescale on it, write it down, and pin it up near your desk, where you see it every day.

5. Be responsive
Develop a reputation for getting back to people very quickly. Once you get into the habit, you'll find that it is easier to deal with something immediately. Most stories need only one sentence from you.

6. Get media trained

Nobody is a natural interviewee. Make sure you know how to perform professionally, and your business will benefit.

7. Become an expert

Offer to speak about your area of expertise. Write articles, give interviews, and make yourself available to answer questions from journalists. Becoming known as a recognised expert in your field is one of the best ways of bringing in new clients

Come to think of it, these things work locally too.

How To Get Into Print

What is the most inefficient way to get your story into print? You can try sending out hundreds of press releases to newspapers and magazines. Yet this is the strategy adopted by hundreds of thousands, if not millions, of companies every day.

Alas, the PR industry is largely to blame, and I speak as a paid-up member of the Chartered Institute of Public Relations. Many of my professional colleagues have convinced their clients that a measure of PR success is the number of press releases sent out each month. That's like saying that a successful darts player is the one who throws most darts at the board.

The only true measure of success in PR is the number of people in your target market who receive, understand and respond to your message. That's it. Sounds a bit like advertising doesn't it? Well here are two differences. Advertising costs a lot of money. Editorial is trusted by many more people than trust advertising, since it's written by an unbiased third party (the journalist). Advertising loses on both counts.

So, having dismissed both press releases and advertising, where do we go from here? Well, hang on a minute. Press releases can be useful, and press advertising still has its place (not least in keeping many local papers solvent).

It is quite possible that your first encounter with a real journalist will be a reporter from the local paper. You may well have cleared this hurdle already, but similar rules apply, whether you are talking to the young and keen reporter from the local Echo or to the business correspondent from The Times.

By the way, don't dismiss local papers as something to move upwards from. They have a very loyal and strong readership, and often franchise stories around their stable of papers. If you tell a good story to a local reporter, it can appear in 20 or more papers over a wide area, and may then be sold on to the national press.

In addition, radio and TV researchers scan newspapers for stories they can broadcast. Getting print coverage should be a very important part of your media strategy.

Many print publications are aimed at a small target market, which may be a local area, particular profession or special interest. In order to make sure your story is printed, you need to do a little research, so that you can provide an angle which will appeal to the readership.

With local papers, of course, the angle is clear. The trick is to make the local link as obvious as possible. Don't worry about it appearing too contrived. As long as the name of the town or village appears in the opening line, the story will be of interest. Have a look at your own local papers to get an idea of how they work. It will be useful to note which reporters write each story, since there may be someone with a particular interest in your type of news. If so, try to speak to them directly.

Also consider whether your story is news or features. News stories are more immediate, and include items such as a new product or service, a reaction to another story, or a protest. They tend to appear on the first few pages (or the back for sports stories), and often include arresting images. Features are lengthier, often with human interest, and usually written some time before publication. They provide the opportunity for a more in-depth story.

Writing It Yourself

Letters to the Editor may also be a way to get your story into print. They can benefit you in a couple of ways.

Firstly, they provide a direct route to an audience, and usually appear exactly as you have written them, giving you the chance to make your points clearly and thoroughly.

Secondly, they may prompt a call from a reporter if they think that the story is newsworthy (or feature-worthy). If you decide to take this route, remember that a brief letter is more likely to be published in full, and you shouldn't try a hard sell, or your words won't appear at all. Most papers now accept letters by email, so you don't even have to buy a stamp.

If you really want to make a name for yourself, and have an hour to spare each week, offer to write a column (this may be known as an *opinion piece* or *op-ed* – short for opposite the editorial page). If you have information that is of special interest to the readers, approach the editor of a journal and make the offer. Explain your expertise, and include an example of your writing.

Don't expect to get paid, though.

Budgets are very tight, and your payback will be the regular publicity that you receive, and contact details at the end of your piece. Be aware that if you make a commitment to a regular column, you will be facing a regular deadline, just like a real journalist. If you are new to this type of thing, find a publication that appears monthly, or even better, quarterly, so you don't over-commit yourself.

For special interest publications, you also need to have an angle, which again should be obvious. If you are struggling to find the connection between your story and the publication, then you probably shouldn't pursue it. You can always resort to the all-purpose statement: Many of my friends are < name of special interest here>, and they tell me that one of the most important issues facing them today is...

Telephone Interviews

Print journalists gather most of their information over the telephone. Although many of them write shorthand, the skill is declining, and you are more likely to be asked if you are happy for the call to be recorded. There is nothing sinister about this, and it makes sense to agree. Remember, though, that there is no such thing as off the record, particularly if your answers have been permanently saved.

Stick to the facts, and don't speculate or exaggerate. In other words, treat it exactly as you would a radio interview.

You should also make a note of the questions you were asked, and the responses you gave. It is unusual to have to challenge a story, but if you do, you will need some evidence. There is a much more important reason for keeping notes, though, and that is to refer back to if the reporter calls again, possibly to clarify a point, or to find out more information. If a colleague takes the call instead of you, it will be extremely useful for them to know what was said.

The great advantage of telephone interviews is that you are able to have all your prompt sheets in front of you, so you can deliver your core message, make all your points, and deal with any awkward questions with consummate ease. At least, you will if you are media-ready (you know who to call if you aren't).

Supply A Story, Not Just Information

Journalists receive hundreds, if not thousands, of press releases each week. Most of them are never read, and those that are nearly always end up in the shredder. That's not because they contain no facts, but because that's all they do contain.

There is no point in sending out a press release about the opening of your latest branch office. Nobody cares.

However, if the new office is powered by a wind turbine on the roof, or is managed by a former nudist camp supervisor, there may well be a story in it. Newspapers and magazines thrive on stories. In fact, that's almost all they consist of.

If you can deliver the type of local and/or human interest which readers love, then your press release will turn out to be very valuable indeed.

Prepare Quotes In Advance

Quotes are always valuable to print journalists, and the more snappy and memorable, the better. You should prepare and practice your quotes before using them in conversation. The reporter will know that you didn't just make them up, but that doesn't matter, since you are helping them add life to the story. Keeping your quotes short and to the point does require some work. As Mark Twain once said in a note attached to a letter to a friend Sorry about the long letter, I didn't have time to write a short one.

Who Do They Work For?

One of the most important things to find out is whether the journalist is staff or freelance, since they are subject to different pressures, and often require information presented in a different way. Staffers work for one publication and will tend to be either young and keen reporters climbing the career ladder, or mature editors and sub-editors who like the security of a regular pay packet. They are more likely to have time to chat to you, attend press events and do lunch. For your part, you should know something about their publication before talking to them.

Freelancers, on the other hand, write for a range of publications, and are more likely to be under pressure, since they are paid by the word. Always ask a freelancer where the article will appear, and if you can help them with anything else they are working on. Become a valued contact for a freelance journalist and they will call you regularly.

Journalists are almost always working to tight deadlines, and they may want to get as much information from you as quickly as possible. However, if they decide to turn the story into a feature, they will often offer to meet you face-to-face, probably with a photographer in tow.

Case Studies

Case studies are also very popular with print journalists, since they can include direct quotes from Real People. It is quite in order for you to supply details of people available for interview, and have personal experience of whatever the story relates to. It is extremely time-consuming for journalists to find case studies, and they will be grateful if you can do the work for them. Any case studies you supply will almost certainly be sympathetic to your viewpoint, so the journalist may also try to find other people for a more balanced view. If you are feeling brave enough, you might supply those contacts too, but this is not your responsibility.

Keeping In Touch

When the interview is over, thank the journalist, make sure you have their contact details, and check when the piece is due to appear. If you are lucky, they may offer to send you the publication with your story in it. This is a very rare event. You will almost certainly have to seek it out yourself. If it is a magazine, you may have to wait several months before the article appears. If you have promised to provide some more details, make sure that you do. Immediately after the interview, make a note of everything you have promised to do, and make sure that you deliver. You will become exactly the kind of contact that journalists love.

Hold The Front Page

Here's a summary of how to get your message in print:

- Customise your message to each newspaper or magazine that you approach.

- Recognise the interest (or prejudice) of the readers of each publication, and use it to your advantage.

- Offer an interview. It is much better than sending out a press release.

- Remember that everything is on the record.

- Follow-up any interview with an email, amplifying any points you need to.

- Never criticise a rival. Say you will have to ask them.

- Don't criticise the reporter if the piece fails to appear. It isn't their fault.

- Keep in touch with reporters from time to time, whether you have a story or not.

Help journalists do their job, and they will help you.

30-Second Print Guide

- ✓ Think about a story, not facts
- ✓ Look for the local angle
- ✓ Case studies are like gold dust – make sure you offer one
- ✓ Letters to the Editor are a great first step
- ✓ Don't advertise, but mention what you do in passing
- ✓ Ask for contact details to be included in the story
- ✓ Try to get a regular slot – a column, or answering readers' questions
- ✓ Be available for quotes at short notice

How To Get On Radio

In most countries, the percentage of people who listen to the radio is in excess of ninety per cent of the adult population. Over 90 per cent! In the UK, that's 45 million people. In the US, that's over 200 million people. Sounds like a good audience to me. It is far more than the number of Internet users (estimated at around 75% in the US and Japan, the highest-using countries, in June 2008 according to Nielsen Netratings). It's almost certainly more than the number of TV viewers too. That's why radio is an excellent medium for you.

Getting on the radio is good for your business. Once again, there is the advertising route or the editorial route. Care to hazard a guess at the one I am going to suggest? Exactly. For the same reasons I mentioned in the previous section, editorial coverage wins every time. If you have a little money to spend, radio advertising can be very cost-effective. However, if you have a little money to spend, there may be even better ways to use it to promote yourself (see other sections of this book).

You should never miss the chance to appear on radio. It doesn't matter what time you are asked to appear, or what station is asking. You should always agree (weddings and funerals excepted, but you'd be amazed how easy it is to rearrange them, while radio interviews are not so flexible). If you refuse, you may never be asked again. If you accept an interview request, and perform well (as you will, having read this book), you will become a contact in the reporter's special notebook. This is worth a great deal to you and your business. You probably won't even have to put yourself out very much, since many interviews are pre-recorded, and can be done over the telephone. It is rare that you will be asked to visit the studio. Most interviews can be conducted from the comfort of your own home. I have lost count of the number of radio interviews I have done early in the morning, wearing a dressing gown and holding a mug of tea (most of them from home, too!)

On radio, you have a great opportunity to sound professional and well-informed, since you can have your notes in front of you as you speak. Of course, I'm sure you sound professional and well-informed all the time, but you can sound especially so on air.

Beware, though, of reading out your messages from a prompt sheet. If the interviewer can tell that you are working from a script, they can turn nasty. It is better to have some notes of your key messages to which you can refer, and re-word according to the questions asked.

Never, ever, take notes into a radio studio.

A few years ago, I was a guest on a BBC Radio Five Live show called *late night live*. I was already in the studio when another guest arrived, and handed two sheets of paper to the presenter, with the words, "You probably won't understand my business, so I've had my PR company prepare a list of questions and model answers for you. I have copies too, so we'll just work through them." This was, of course, a huge error.

The presenter smiled, and tore the crib sheets into confetti. Throwing the shards over the hapless guest as the ON AIR light came on, the presenter tore into him with a series of tough questions that left the guest reeling and speechless. It was like watching a lion bringing down a gazelle. The guest left the studio shattered, and I don't recall hearing him on radio again to this day.

It is never a wise move to patronise a radio presenter.

You should make sure that you smile on radio. It will change the tone of your voice, and make your listeners more receptive. Of course, there are some subjects where humour would not be an appropriate emotion, but if you are promoting your business you should be able to talk about the lighter side. Not only does it make you sound more engaging, if you can generate a good laugh, the next thing you say will be listened to more closely, as all good speakers know.

Radio is an interesting medium. Unlike print or TV, users (listeners) rarely give it their full attention. When the radio is on, people may be preparing a meal, driving to or from work, relaxing in the bath, or simply doing nothing much. That means your message has to be a strong one to interrupt what they are doing and make them think I must listen to that.

3 Tips For Getting On Radio

If you want to be on radio, here's a three-point plan to follow.

1. Listen To The Radio

I know, how hard is that? Make sure you have a pen and paper handy. Listen to a show that you'd like to be on. If you're a business, aim for the shows when people have time to listen, such as late evening.

The Breakfast and Drivetime shows are no use, since listeners are doing something else, and not really paying full attention.

The best time to listen depends on the audience you want to reach. The middle of the day is best for stay-at-home types, including the millions of people who now work from home.

If you are trying to attract the attention of large corporations, then aim for mid to late evening, when people are home and relaxing, and are liable to pay much more attention to your message. Not only that, you are likely to be given more air time, since there is less need to include regular news, weather and travel updates.

Listen for about an hour, and make notes of when you listen, the name of the presenter, who the guests are, and the topics discussed. Include everything you hear (including interviews and news items). Make copious notes, since you will need them in the next two stages of the process.

2. Make A Connection

Spend a little time reviewing your notes, looking for a link between what you hear and your business. For example, if you have an IT business and you hear the presenter mention that they have real problems with technology, that's a connection. You may find several points of connection, so consider carefully which is the one that you want to pursue. If you can't make any connection at all, it's time to listen again, maybe to a dedicated business show.

Now take a sheet of paper to use as a prompt sheet in the final stage of the process.

First, write down how you will introduce yourself (name and company). This may sound obvious, but it is important to be able to make your case as convincingly as possible, and stumbling over your introduction will not impress anyone.

Then in clear, concise terms, write down the name of the show, time and date and presenter.

Then, in a couple of sentences, summarise the connection. Take care over preparing this sheet, since you may only get one opportunity to get your message across to the right person.

3. Make The Call

With your notes in hand, including the connection you noted, phone the radio station and ask to speak to the station's deputy editor. They receive fewer calls than the editor, and they are keener to make their mark, so are liable to be more responsive. There is no point speaking to the show's presenter, since they don't book guests. When you get through, explain who you are, and your connection. Offer to come into the station for a chat.

You may not be invited on air straight away. However, if you have made a convincing case, your chances of getting on the station are high. Very few people make this kind of approach to a radio station, and they are generally very receptive, since finding good guests is often a difficult task.

If you follow those three steps, in every detail, you will find that in most cases you are invited to appear on air. That's the time you need media coaching (but that's another book altogether).

Live On Air

The first time that you enter a radio studio, you will probably find it much smaller than you expect. You will be taken into the studio just before your interview, and shown where to sit. There will be a microphone on the table, and a set of headphones (often called *cans*). There is no need to put these on unless you are directed to do so, since the interviewer is probably sitting just across the desk. They will be wearing headphones, so that the producer and technical operator can speak to them. Even if you put the headphones on, you won't hear the people in the control room.

If you are asked to put headphones on, it will be to hear someone from a remote location, or to listen to a recording. You probably won't be told, but there is a volume control at the end of the headphone lead, sometimes hidden just under the desk. Adjust the volume to suit yourself. You will also see a button on the desk in front of you marked *Cough* or *PTM (Push To Mute)*. Holding down the button turns your microphone off, should you need to clear your throat.

When the red light is on, the studio is live, and anything you say may be picked up by the microphones.

Try to avoid rustling papers, swinging to and fro in your squeaky chair, or making any whispered asides. You may see various characters – news readers, sports correspondents and the like – entering and leaving the studio while the red light is shining. They (usually) know how to keep quiet. You should follow the instructions of whoever escorts you in and out.

Many radio studios have TV monitors tuned to news stations or information services. They are there to help the presenter keep up-to-date with breaking news. Try to ignore them. I remember being in a studio with another guest who was so mesmerised by a football match on one of the screens that he didn't hear his introduction, and was completely confused as he tried to answer the first half-heard question.

"I didn't have time to make my point!"

Alas, I've heard that phrase many times over the years. Remarkably, it often comes from the lips of people who consider themselves to be great communicators.

Of course, it isn't true. You always have time to make your point on radio, but you have to be concise. You have to prepare a phrase well before the interview, and find a way of delivering it. I've talked about your core message many times, but I cannot over-stress its importance. However good you are, you should never try to wing it without any forethought. You may get away with it, but you probably won't deliver that memorable message.

Never go into an interview without a short, pithy phrase that you can deliver in less than 10 seconds. If you find yourself with plenty of time, simply use the phrase several times in your answers.

On the occasion when the interviewer says to you, "I must ask you to be very brief, we have only a few seconds before the news," you'll still have plenty of time to get your message across.

It Ain't Over 'Til It's Over

Imagine the scene; you are called to a radio studio to do a pre-recorded interview. You plan carefully, have a good core message, and perform well, since the reporter doesn't ask any of the difficult questions you feared. The interview finishes, and the interviewer leans over, shakes your hand, and thanks you for your time. You thank them in return, and say how glad you were that they avoided that particularly awkward topic.

So far so good?

Hang on.

The interviewer puts a hand to their headphones and the other hand towards you, gesturing you to sit down again.

"I'm sorry," they say. "There was a problem with the recording. Do you mind if we do it again?"

Of course you don't mind, thinking it will be even easier second time around. You smile and wait for the first question, which, to your acute embarrassment, is on the topic you wanted to avoid.

Of course, there was no problem with the first recording. You made the error of assuming that everything was over. It wasn't. Next time, wait until you are well clear of microphones before you analyse the interview.

30-Second Radio Guide

- ✓ Find out about the station and the show in advance
- ✓ Plan your message well in advance – and stick to it
- ✓ Follow the instructions from the station staff
- ✓ Assume that the microphones are always on
- ✓ Get your core message in early
- ✓ Repeat your core message at the end
- ✓ Leave your contact details
- ✓ Jot down your notes as soon as the interview is over

How To Get On TV

Getting directly on to TV is not easy. There is no great trick to it, either, since it relies on one of two things (sometimes both) – hard work and a good reputation.

The first if these is obviously the most important, since without it, you won't achieve the second. Many guests on TV shows are either already known to the show's producer and editor, or are recommended because of their prominence in print or on radio.

You should also ask yourself, "Why do I want to be on TV?"

Since it is more time-consuming than radio or print (you can often be interviewed over the phone from your desk), and you are likely to be on air for less time, why do it at all? If it is purely from an egotistical point of view, forget it. There are better ways to spend your time. However, if it is part of your overall PR strategy, and has obvious benefits, then read the rest of this section to improve your chances of getting on TV.

Firstly, you can make sure that you are on one of the directories that journalists search for **experts**. These include: **www.expertsources.co.uk**, **www.presschoice.com**, and **www.findatvexpert.com**

The first two sites are mainly news-related, the third is more for experts who want to appear in a longer show, or even a series. All charge a small subscription, but are well worth it.

Secondly, you can respond to **requests** put out by TV channels or production companies. These are a bit more arbitrary, but can lead to you getting noticed by TV production companies.

Thirdly, you can make **a direct pitch** (as detailed for radio). You may be lucky. Thousands aren't.

In The TV Studio

TV studios can be daunting places for newcomers. There is a lot of technology, bright lights, and random activity going on, with several people apparently talking to themselves. Despite the glossy appearance on screen, much of the furniture is held together with sticky tape and string, as you will see when you sit behind it. I recall being on a breakfast TV show, behind a table with an appetising bowl of fruit and a glass of orange juice. As I sat down, the floor manager said to me, "Don't drink the orange juice, it's coloured water. And the fruit is plastic."

If you have a dry throat, ask for some (real) water. Have some throat sweets handy. If you find that your mouth still gets dry, you can use the old actor's trick. Gently nip the inside of your cheek with your teeth, and you will find that your mouth becomes moist. Don't overdo it by biting too hard, since that will bring tears to your eyes as well.

There will be TV monitors around, showing various images.

Don't look at them.

There will be cameras moving around.

Don't look at them.

There will be a scrolling autocue script for the presenter to read.

Don't look at it.

Instead, look at the interviewer and forget everything else.

When you are introduced, smile. Don't look shifty. Say hello and nod. If they make a mistake over your name or title, correct them politely. Remember that you will need to be *miked-up*. The presenter will wear an ear piece. If they don't pay attention to you before the interview, bear in mind they may be receiving instructions from the gallery.

Focus on your message, and do what you are told by the floor manager.

It will all be over before you know it.

Time Is Money

Television time is expensive. Very expensive.

A two-minute advert in prime time television can cost hundreds of thousands of pounds (dollars, euros or whatever). If you have the opportunity to be interviewed for a couple of minutes on a prime-time show, remember just what that opportunity is worth. If you had to pay for the privilege, you would make every second count, wouldn't you?

Although the interview is free, you should still be aware of its value to you. Of course, that doesn't mean you should treat it like an advert, and promote your products or services. You would never be asked again. It does mean that you should plan your message well in advance, choose your words with care, and deliver a well-crafted performance.

Make sure that you understand why you are being interviewed. Of all the people who could have been called, your name was top (OK maybe everyone else was away, but never mind that now).

You should provide information which is useful, relevant to the viewers, and demonstrates your knowledge of the topic. As with a speech, if you have nothing useful to say, then pass the opportunity on to someone else.

Be sure that when the interview is over, you can say to yourself, "Yes, that was worth it".

Look The Part

As I travel the world, I watch TV interviews, sometimes in a language I don't fully understand. However, I can often tell whether the interviewee is coming across well simply by checking their appearance. While your words are of great importance (don't believe that popular misconception that words convey only 7% of meaning), appearance is important too.

In addition to how you are perceived by others, your appearance can affect how you feel. In order to deliver a confident performance, you need to feel good about yourself, and only you can be the judge of that. Even if others tell you you look fine, you will know whether you are happy with your appearance.

Somewhat surprisingly, your appearance is important on radio too. For the reason just mentioned: if you are feeling good about yourself, you will perform better. Not only that, but the way that you look will affect how radio interviewers treat you. If you are speaking on behalf of a professional body, such as a group of lawyers, you will not be taken so seriously if you arrive at the studios wearing jeans and a t-shirt. On the other hand, if you are an eco-warrior, a three-piece pinstripe suit may be inappropriate.

Take as much care over your appearance as your message, and make sure they work in harmony.

Using Props

If you want to bring something into the studio with you – a new product that you are discussing, or your latest book – always ask first.

The producer will be concerned about camera shots, and since they can't talk to you directly, they may ask the interviewer to take the object from you, so that they can show it to the camera.

If you are pre-recording an interview, you may have the advantage of a rehearsal with a prop. This will allow you to practice the camera shots in advance.

Of course, things still may not go to plan. For some years, I had a regular slot as a technology expert on a weekly TV show. Much of the show was devoted to new technology, which I would explain to the presenter. We often used to encounter what Denis Norden used to call the OOPS effect (Objects Only Perform Sometimes). If your demonstration goes horribly wrong, as mine did from time to time, the only thing to do is to make a joke of it and explain what it should have done.

In general, my advice would be to avoid props.

The Eyes Have It

When you are being interviewed (or, to be fair, whenever you are communicating), eye contact is very important.

You should try to make eye contact with your interviewer the whole time.

If you find this disconcerting, you can try focusing on the tip of their nose, or just above their eyebrows. No-one will notice, and it's only for a few minutes.

Don't be too put off if your interviewer seems distracted, and looks away while you are answering. It is likely that they will be listening to the voice of their producer (and possibly several other advisors) in their earpiece. It's nothing personal. It's probably just as well that you can't hear what is being said, too.

If you are taking part in a down-the-line interview (we've talked about those before), then eye contact is critical. However, there is no-one to look at, simply a camera lens. Whether you find this easier or more difficult is a matter of personal taste, but it is a media skill you need to master.

Most importantly, keep your gaze upward. Looking down can indicate uncertainty, or a lack of self-esteem. My father, an engineer, used to tell a joke:

> How can you tell an extroverted engineer from an introverted engineer?
>
> An extroverted engineer looks at *your* shoes.

Not Being There

You may well be asked to do a TV interview with a presenter in a remote location. These down-the-line interviews can be tough to do, since there is no-one there with you, and you have to do a fair amount of set-up work yourself. Even in Broadcasting House in London, the original home of the BBC, you may be given a key to the remote studio, shown the way, and left to it. If you are luckier, you will be helped by a technician, who will set everything up for you before the interview starts.

Your focus will be the camera that is pointing at you. You need to look directly at it for the duration of your interview. If you look away, even for a moment, the viewer will perceive you as being less than totally honest, since it will appear to them that you can't look them in the eye.

The trick to this type of interview, then, is to keep looking at the lens. Speaking to an inanimate object is not easy. For this reason, most presenters will imagine that they are talking to a trusted friend on the other side of the lens. If you can visualise a colleague, friend or family member that you enjoy talking to, imagine that you are speaking to them, and them alone, through the lens in front of you.

You will hear the interviewer's voice through a speaker. Don't look to where the voice is coming from, but keep focusing on the camera. If there is a monitor in the room, showing the interviewer in vision, it is almost impossible to ignore it. What you can do before the interviewer is to ask the technician if you can turn it off or turn it away from you. As a last resort, throw your coat over it.

Keep your gaze steady. It will only be for a few minutes. Finally, don't forget that you may be in sound and vision, and possibly recorded, before the interview starts. Don't make any unguarded remarks, even in jest.

30-Second TV Guide

- ✓ Prepare well in advance
- ✓ Take your notes with you, but tuck them out of sight
- ✓ Think about your appearance, and ask someone to check you over
- ✓ Arrive in plenty of time
- ✓ If you need to use the toilet or have a drink, do it before you sit in the green room
- ✓ Be ready for an instant call
- ✓ Follow the floor manager's instructions
- ✓ Look at the interviewer, not the camera
- ✓ Get your core message in early
- ✓ Stay still until you are told to move
- ✓ Record your impressions

Publicity Stunts

You can generate a huge amount of publicity for very little expense with a well-planned publicity stunt. Of course, however clever and creative you are, there is no point setting up a stunt unless you can get press coverage. There is no Field of Dreams for stunts – if you build it, they will not come unless you tell them to.

A well-planned and skilfully-executed stunt will have certain characteristics

1. High news value

2. Good timing

3. A strong link to the product or service being promoted

4. A visual element

5. Able to be summarised in a line

6. Memorable

Whether it's Britney kissing Madonna at the MTV Awards, or Richard Branson dressing as an Air Stewardess to promote Virgin Atlantic, good stunts tick all the boxes. Let's look at the characteristics in more detail.

1) High News Value – What's The Story?

Reporters have a nose for news. You need to develop the same thing, by working out what the story is. World record attempts are always popular, especially if there is a great photo opportunity. If you are a small organisation, use the David and Goliath approach, and show how you compare favourably with large companies. On the other hand, if you are a huge company, demonstrate your humble credentials by doing something that shows how much you care about your customers.

2) Good Timing

If you want your stunt to appear on the Six O'clock News, then plan it for 11 o'clock in the morning. Any later, and there may not be time to film it and edit the package for the early evening news. If you want print coverage, then consider the deadlines of newspapers. For a weekly paper, plan the stunt at least two days in advance of publication day. Don't waste your time pitching a stunt to a magazine, since their lead times are much too long, and they don't want to print old news.

3) A Strong Link To The Product Or Service

This seems obvious, but some stunts become so complex that they develop a life of their own, and people only remember the stunt, not the purpose of it. It's like watching a very clever TV advert, and then trying to recall the product a day or two later (oddly, these ads often win awards). Always remember the purpose of the stunt, and make sure that the message comes through loud and clear.

4) A Visual Element

You must ensure that there is a photo opportunity. It may be that the only media interest is from a photographer, so you need to make sure there is an arresting image. If all else fails, and no media turn up, take photos yourself for later distribution. Pictures with crowds of people enjoying themselves, and engaged in some activity, are the ones you are looking for. If you can get the name of your company in the picture (not too blatant, but visible), then so much the better.

5) Able To Be Summarised In A Line

It should be easy for a journalist to write about your stunt. It must be obvious what is going on. If it isn't clear pictorially, there must be a simple message that can be used in a headline. Not only must it be simple, it must be concise and relevant to the likely audience. You know what I mean.

6) Memorable

Of course your stunt has to be memorable, and have a memorable message. The true test of a great stunt is when you hear it being discussed weeks later. The best stunts of all are talked about for years. However, if no-one can remember the name of the product or service (see above), then the impact is lost.

30-Second Publicity Stunt Guide

- ✓ Contact the press early
- ✓ Time your stunt to fit in with deadlines
- ✓ Make it easy to get to
- ✓ Make sure it is captured on video or photos
- ✓ Keep it relevant
- ✓ Make it visual
- ✓ Put the video/pictures on the Internet (many a stunt has taken off via a YouTube video)

Blogging

Blogging is just like writing a diary, except that anyone on the Internet can read it. For some people, blogging has become almost a way of life, defining themselves as bloggers above all else. However, there are millions of blogs, most of them unread. So why bother? There are several reasons...

4 Good Reasons To Blog

Reason 1: Blogs that provide useful advice will be followed by potential customers, who will refer them on to their friends.

It's another way of raising your profile and promoting your brand. If you are seen as an expert who constantly provides practical advice, you will become trusted, and people buy from those they trust. If your blog becomes known as a centre of expertise and debate for your sector, you will benefit from the credibility that it gives, as well as receiving valuable ideas and feedback. Some of the most popular blogs are read by tens of thousands of people, and can act as opinion formers within an industry. Because of the simplicity and speed of production, news can break on a blog before it is seen or heard anywhere else. This is part of the phenomenon known as citizen journalism.

But there is a downside too. Because the majority of blogs are the work of one person, they may consist of opinions or rumours masquerading as verified facts. If your blog is to be seen as credible, you should take as much care as a journalist publishing an article in a magazine, particularly since the laws of libel still apply.

Reason 2: You can use your blog not only to promote your brand, but also to protect it.

If a crisis occurs, you need to establish yourself as the main source of information. Your blog can act as a focus for customers and journalists alike. Not only that, if you allow comments (as you should, in my view), you will see instantly the concerns that are being raised, and be able to move quickly to deal with them. However, don't feel the need to respond personally to every critical comment on your blog. You will find that other readers will often post comments that deal with the issue for you. In addition, there are some mischievous individuals who will post provocative comments simply to start a debate, which if you enter it, you will never win. You do need to keep an eye out for obscene or potentially libellous comments, however, and delete them as soon as you can.

Reason 3: Blogger.com is owned by Google.

This means that it is a good way of **increasing your visibility** in the world's most used search engine. However, beware of treating your blog as simply a way to get a higher Google rating by filling it with links, Google are wise to that trick. In addition, your rating in a search engine is becoming less important, as web users become more sophisticated and knowledgeable, and will key in your site address directly. That doesn't mean you have to use blogger.com. Other blogging platforms offer different features as you'll see later.

Reason 4: Regular blogging gets you into the habit of writing often, which is essential if you ever want to write that book.

For example, let's assume you write a blog every day of 250 words. Ten blogs (2,500 words) can be pulled together into a special report. Four special reports (10,000 words) make a good sized e-book (delivered electronically, like a word-processing file). Four e-books (40,000 words) make a real book. If you've been paying attention, you will realise that in 10 x 4 x 4 days (160 days, or about six months, allowing for a bit if time off), you can have written a book, by doing nothing more than blogging. So, if you write a daily blog of 250 words, you can turn out two books a year.

What should I put in my blog? The most obvious answer is engaging content.

If you want people to leave with a good impression, you must provide something of value. Your blog has to be interesting, but more importantly, must give the reader something they can use, or something they can think about. You can include video, pictures, audio or text, but all of it needs to be there for a reason. It is very important, as in all forms of communication, to consider the needs of your audience. However fascinating you may find pictures of pre-war doorstops, unless you have an audience that likes them too, it is pointless including them in your blog.

The easiest way to find out what works for your audience is to watch the comments you receive. They will tell you what is important to your readers, and you should heed what they say.

If people read blogs at all, it is unlikely that they will pay attention to more than five on a regular basis. Given the choice of millions, you need to think carefully about how you can make your blog a must-read.

Engaging content is valuable, inspiring or thought-provoking (hopefully all three). You must be interested in what you write, otherwise your readers will move on. Ideally, you should not be just interested, but passionate. Your passion will come through in the way you express yourself, and you will develop a loyal following. Despite the mention of Google above, never forget that you are writing a blog for real people to read, not for search engines to crawl over.

Check your content carefully for spelling and grammar before you post it. I don't know about you, but when I find simple spelling errors, or badly-written sentences, I am distracted from the meaning of the content. Ideally, ask someone to proof-read your postings for you. If you can't find anyone handy, try the trick of reading them out loud. You will be surprised at how easy it is to spot any errors.

Give yourself plenty of time to write your blog postings. A post which has been dashed off in a hurry will be obvious, and can indicate a lack of respect for your readers. If you are keen to post some breaking news, you can always add a couple of sentences to make your point, and indicate that you will expand the post when you have more time, and more information.

Remember that some people will be visiting your blog for the first time, and you should offer them something too. I recommend that you create a *Guide For First-Timers*, including links to important posts, and outlining your philosophy. Make sure that this guide is visible on every page of your blog by including a box about it in the sidebar. It's easy to do this if you look at the Tools option, and will prove very valuable to you.

To help all readers, both new and experienced, to navigate your blog, you can create another box in the sidebar which links to popular posts, or those you are particularly proud of. This will help people to understand your point of view, and will save them from having to search for the really good stuff (yes, I know, it's all good stuff, but some of it, I'm sure, is especially brilliant)

Within your blog posts, include links to other posts, other sites, or definitions of terms that may not be obvious. Your readers will really appreciate this.

What About Look And Feel?

You will have the choice of some basic designs from your blog host (usually Blogger or Wordpress). However, there are plenty of sites that will allow you to customise the appearance of your blog, and for a small fee, you can have a design made to order. Whether you go this far is up to you, but there if you have recognisable logo, font or colours, your blog should show them.

Do I Have To Write My Blog Myself?

If you're busy, you may consider employing someone else to write blog posts for you. There are a number of large corporations that have gone down this route. A note of caution – if your ghost-writer is pretending to be you, and the subterfuge is discovered, it could be very bad PR. The simple rule I suggest is that if it has your name on it, the words should be yours, even if they are dictated by you, rather than typed in. If it is a corporate blog, it doesn't matter so much, but putting by-lines on each posting is a nice touch.

Can I Make Money From My Blog?

In short, no. If you want to use your blog as a direct money-making operation, you have the wrong book in your hand. Indirectly, your blog can lead to a more profitable business, by establishing you as an expert, but don't expect people to pay for blog content. I would also advise against having relevant adverts down the side of your blog, since they not only distract from the content, they produce very small returns.

One More Thing

Don't call it a blog, since that can put people off. I call my blog *The Media Coach Report*. It sounds friendlier, and attracts more readers.

30-Second Blogging Guide

- ✓ Blog every day (OK, you can take Sunday off)
- ✓ Blog early in the day to get it done
- ✓ Link to it from your site
- ✓ Encourage people to comment
- ✓ Add extra features (such as video links and Twitter feeds)
- ✓ Use pictures occasionally
- ✓ Think about your audience – write for them
- ✓ If you don't enjoy writing it, don't do it

Social Media Principles

Hundreds of social networking sites exist, from LinkedIn to Facebook. To explain how to use each of them is beyond the scope of this guide. Their great advantage is that many of them can be used for free.

Each social network has its own advantages and disadvantages, with some being more business-orientated, and some definitely just social. If you intend to use social networks as part of your PR strategy, focus on just one initially, and raise your profile within it, by commenting, blogging and posting useful links. As you become more well-known, people will invite you to join them on other networks.

But beware, this type of thing can become addictive. Set yourself limits for the time you spend on a social network, and be strict about it. Treat it like a trip to the coffee machine for a chat, rather than the main point of your day. Have fun, but remember that you are also there to benefit your business.

How Do I Get Started?

If, dear reader, you are daunted by the thought of having to learn how to use social media to help your business, here are a few baby steps to get you started:

- Focus on just one social network at a time

- Pick a place where your customers are already

- Watch the conversations and read the comments

- Offer something of value, such as advice, a contact or a link

- Be social – don't just talk about your business

- Don't sell – just be there, and be helpful

- Don't worry about return on investment – the worst that can happen is that you had a few hours of fun

Are We Human, Or Are We Chancers?

I don't know about you, but I like to have a relationship with a real person, not a machine. On lots of social networks, including Facebook and Twitter, I see more and more automated messages, whether as replies, or even worse, as automatic Tweets about what's happening on news sites, or related to topics that the sender has pre-selected by keywords.

Frankly, I find the whole thing rude. So I block the senders, a habit I'm having to indulge in several times a day on Twitter, where some users – presumably without knowing it – send up to 30 news-related Tweets at exactly the same time.

You'd think that people who use social media regularly would know better than to take a chance on losing followers. Fewer, more personal, messages, would be much more effective. Sending hundreds of soulless ones is not raising your profile, it's just silly. So are you human, or are you a chancer?

Tell People What You Think

There's a clue in the name Social Media (no, not media). You will have much greater success if you tell people your views, get involved in debates, and offer opinions on current topics. Many people fear that if they express an opinion, they might offend someone, and lose a potential customer. The reverse is true. Your clients and customers want to know how you think, and why you are saying things. Naturally, there will be some people who disagree with you, but there will also be people who love you.

If you try to remain safe by simply posting links to news sites, or re-sending other people's opinions, you will struggle to build up your own following. Being seen as boring is only one step from being ignored. OK, you can go too far the other way, and disagree with people just for the sake of it, or express very controversial views. That's not necessary.

Simply state your case, back it up with reasons, and see how people respond. You'll find that you become the person that others recommend, and your influence and reputation will grow.

Do As You Would Be Done By

It's a given that you should always offer help to others when you are using social networking sites. Of course, it's fine to ask for help too. Alas, there are some social networkers who only ever ask for advice, and never give anything back. Of course, that's not just a feature of social networks. All of us know contacts who only ever take from us (and presumably they don't remain contacts for long).

However, on sites like Linkedin and Facebook, the impact of being a taker rather than a giver is more apparent. Because replies and comments are often public, your behaviour towards others is seen by the community at large. Just as being helpful will enhance your reputation, being unhelpful will damage it.

So take the initiative. Don't just wait to be asked for advice, but post articles and features which others will find useful. Your reputation and influence will grow, and as a result, business will come to you.

Change Your Thinking

When you create messages on social networking sites, you may need to change the way you think about information. Here are a few things to think about:

- Think collaboration, not competition. It's how you help that matters.

- Think in headlines, or short phrases, like Twitter

- Think about your audience. It's not what you know, it's what they want to hear

- Think carefully. Your message can be misinterpreted. Consider how it might be perceived

- Think permanence. There's a site that takes snapshots of the Internet on a regular basis. Deleting messages doesn't hide them completely.

- Think twice. Don't send a message in haste (see above)

How To Be Helpful

I've mentioned before the prime rule of social networking - be helpful. Here are a few ways that you can help your fellow networkers:

1) Run **real-time advice clinics** on Twitter. I do this when I have some free time between meetings. In 30 minutes you can answer a dozen questions, which are not only helpful to the questioner, but also appear in the public stream, so others can see your expertise.

2) Publish **top tips lists** on your blog or Facebook page. If you do this regularly, you will find people asking to re-publish them. Say yes, provided they include a live link back to your site.

3) **Answer other people's questions**. Offer direct help, or connect them to an expert who can help them. Never bluff. Only offer help if you know the answer. OK - which one of those will you do today?

30-Second Social Media Guide

✓ Don't join more networks than you can cope with

✓ Offer valuable advice, not just marketing

✓ Give more than you expect to receive

✓ Use the networks regularly

✓ Try to get to some face-to-face events too

✓ Make your profile interesting

✓ Always publish a recent picture, in business dress

✓ Be polite

✓ Offer to help newcomers

✓ If you don't; like something or someone, move on, don't complain

✓ Join groups and participate in debates

✓ Don't expect instant results

Alan Stevens

Twitter

Although there are several microblogs, Twitter – **www.twitter.com** – is by far the most popular, with millions of users worldwide. In concept, it is very simple. The tagline is, "What are you doing?" and you can type in up to 140 characters to answer the question. Your message, *Tweet* can be input via a website or a mobile phone.

Other users can subscribe to your 'feed' or stream of messages, to become 'followers', and see what you are doing. You can choose to follow other users too, to see what they are up to.

Why Has Twitter Become So Popular, And Why Is It Useful?

For one thing, it is another way of raising your profile in a pool of potential customers. However, if you treat it as just a marketing tool, your followers will rapidly drift away.

The real value of Twitter is in creating and maintaining relationships. Many of my followers are people that I know personally, but struggle to keep in touch with. Twitter gives me the chance to maintain contact. It is also useful on a professional level, to keep abreast of developments in your field of expertise.

Despite the 140 character limit, Tweets can be used to ask questions, give advice, provide links to other sites. The most successful users mix up their Tweets to include personal information, handy links, and the occasional piece of self-promotion.

You need to be wary, since, just like everywhere else on the Web, people are not always who they appear to be. There are many fake celebrities, but some genuine ones, should you be interested in the minutiae of their lives.

There are many applications and add-ons for Twitter. Every day, more seem to appear, so I won't list them here. The best advice is to try it out. It isn't for everyone, but if you use it well, the results are astonishing.

What's The Point?

When I talk to people about how I use social media such as Twitter, they sometimes ask, "What's the point of telling people what you had for lunch?" I tend to agree with them. However, I do sometimes tell people what I had for lunch. I also tell people what I think about various media topics. I answer questions about PR. I post links to my blog and my Internet radio show.

In short, I mix up my messages, so that web users see me as a real person, not just a company that wants their business. People like to do business with other people that they know, like and trust. Showing them that you have other things in your life outside business helps that relationship to develop.

That's the point.

Coming In To Land From Twitter

A landing page is a page on your website that serves a couple of purposes. Firstly, it helps you to track where visitors come from (since the link to that page will appear in only one place). Secondly, it helps your visitor to understand what the site is all about, bearing in mind where they came from. Let me explain.

You can put a link in your profile (though many people don't). It's easy to create a special landing page for Twitter arrivals. That's exactly what I do on my website. I explain my policy for following back, and what people can expect from me. It's only polite, in my view. Don't forget to put some Google Analytics code on it too.

Watch The Trends

The simple rule of business is to sell what people are buying. It pays (literally) to keep an eye on what topics people are interested in, so that you can relate your selling copy to it.

There are some web tools that help you monitor trends. One of the easiest to keep an eye on is Trending Topics on Twitter. These are listed on the right-hand side of the page, under the search box. The top ten most-used terms are displayed as links, so that you can click on them and watch the discussions happening. They probably won't come as much of a surprise, but if your market includes Twitter users, it could be very useful to know what they are talking about.

71

Who Do I Know Who Knows Someone?

Social networking is not just about who you know. It's much more about who they know. For example, I have around 4,000 Twitter followers. Assuming an average of 500 followers for each of them, I can reach two million people in two steps. It's this, in my opinion, that is making Twitter 'the collective brain of the planet'. Once, I used to turn to Google if I had a question I couldn't answer. Now I turn to Twitter. In the one week alone, It has helped me find the source of an obscure quote, located a cosy bed and breakfast in Sedona, Arizona, and allowed me to set up an interview with an innovative PR company. All of the responses came back within ten minutes.

It's not who you know, it's who they know (and what they know, too).

But What Should I Do On Twitter?

I often hear that question asked. So I turn it around: "What would you like people to do for you on Twitter?"

The answer is usually immediate: "Offer me help, and provide me with useful contacts." Exactly!

So that's what you have to do on social networks. If you know what your friends and followers want, and you provide it to them, you have understood the strategy. In short, provide value.

In other words, offer advice if you can, connect people, and upload useful information. The idea of keeping all your knowledge to yourself until someone pays you for it doesn't work in social media. However, the more you give away, the more people will value your advice, and some of them really will be prepared to pay for it.

Don't expect people to reciprocate, either. A thank you is always welcome, but you don't have to return a favour immediately. If you stick with it, the returns will come.

Quality, Not Quantity

Whatever social network you use, there is always the temptation to compare yourself with other users, to see how many friends or followers they have. Some people feel inadequate when they look at Stephen Fry's Twitter account, and see that he has over 300,000 people in tow. If that's your feeling, then stop worrying now. The one with the most followers is not necessarily the winner.

Remember that connecting with people is not just having mutual links on the Internet. That's completely useless unless you can build a relationship with them. The most successful social networkers often end up having face-to-face meetings with people they are linked to online, and it is that personal contact that finally leads to a sale or cooperation. You can't do that with 300,000 people.

OK, there are some people who play the numbers game. It can work if you are selling a commodity. But it is much harder to build trust at a distance, and people buy from people they trust. If you provide a service, then use social networking as part of the introductory process, not as a game of numbers.

30-Second Twitter Guide

- ✓ Don't over-promote. Twitter is not just a marketing tool
- ✓ Be helpful. Offer advice and useful links
- ✓ Don't stay on Twitter all day. Treat it like a visit to the coffee machine
- ✓ Ask questions, get involved in debates
- ✓ Be polite
- ✓ Be yourself. Never pretend to be someone else
- ✓ If you want to send something sensitive, send a direct message
- ✓ Never swear
- ✓ Have fun

LinkedIn

LinkedIn – **www.linkedin.com** – is a social networking site with a strong business bias. It can be an extremely useful tool in your PR strategy. There are millions of potential contacts who may be receptive to your message. As you build your network, be aware that you need to keep adding value to your contacts by offering them advice, pointing them to useful articles, and engaging them in discussions.

One valuable feature is the 'Groups'. You can create your own group on any topic, and invite contacts to join. For example, if you publish a book, create a LinkedIn group, and encourage participants to discuss the issues in your book. Don't forget that if you establish such a community, you need to visit often, in order to respond to any queries, and keep an eye on what is being said.

Look for existing groups in your area of expertise and join them. It's probably a good idea to request only weekly updates, otherwise your inbox will fill up rapidly with email notifications.

To make new connections, use the 'search' feature, and concentrate on second-level followers, with whom you share a mutual friend. When you ask for a connection, the system allows you to send a message to the intermediary. Use that option, since a trusted friend is one of the best ways to encourage people to connect. You can search based on any text in the profiles, but one of the best techniques is to use a combination of location and job title (For example, *HR Managers in Manchester*). Don't overlook the fact that a significant number of journalists use LinkedIn, so include terms like *editor* and *correspondent* in your searches too. As ever, don't pester people unnecessarily, and only offer to make a connection if it is in your mutual interest (and preferably more valuable to them than to you).

If you're trying to find a journalist, or a source of information, LinkedIn's 'answers' feature is also very useful. You can ask questions or become involved in debates. If you answer a few questions before asking any, you will be seen as an expert who needs information rather than someone trying to pitch a story. It's the old rule (which I'm sure your mother taught you) of giving more than you expect to receive.

30-Second LinkedIn Guide

- ✓ Include as much information as possible about yourself
- ✓ Use your primary contacts to introduce you to second-level contacts
- ✓ Use the Groups feature
- ✓ Answer and pose questions
- ✓ Find contacts to meet wherever your business takes you by using the search feature
- ✓ Don't over-promote yourself
- ✓ Keep it professional – LinkedIn is business-oriented

Alan Stevens

Facebook

Facebook — **www.facebook.com** — has an image of being a purely social network. Don't be fooled. It can be a very useful tool in your PR kit. OK, it's not the ideal place to be if your market is business to business. However, Facebook is now growing up, and the owners clearly have Twitter in their sights. More and more businesses are now making use of Facebook to get their message to a wider audience, so you should be there too.

Facebook groups exists to cater for every interest, and there are some excellent ones which discuss PR and Marketing issues. Provided you don't appear too needy, you can find some excellent advice and help. You can also join groups where your customers are likely to be, but as ever, don't try to sell too hard, otherwise you will be ignored.

Using Facebook's 'share' function, you can offer a continual feed of updates and information to your network of friends. For example, if you appear on radio or television, you should share this news with your connections. You can also share links and news that are relevant to your industry, making yourself a hub of information, and positioning yourself as a person in the know.

Facebook also has some great features for promoting events, so if you have a product launch, or a performance that would interest your followers, encourage them to come along by sending out invitations. Send a couple of reminders just prior to the event, but don't bombard people with information.

You may also connect with reporters and bloggers, who may one day feature your information. As with all relationships of this type, make sure that you offer them links and tips about information likely to be of interest to them which is not your own. It's important, though, to determine whether they use Facebook for business or personal reasons (or maybe both). It's possible that another method of communication is better for business use, even though they are your friend on Facebook.

30-Second Facebook Guide

- ✓ Link your Twitter and Facebook updates together (and others too, using a service such as PingFM – **www.ping.fm**)
- ✓ Use it to promote events
- ✓ Encourage people to become friends or fans
- ✓ Consider separate (but linked) accounts for personal and business use
- ✓ Post pictures, audio and video
- ✓ Respond to other's comments on your wall
- ✓ Share outside information and links

Alan Stevens

Ezines

Newsletters have been around for hundreds of years in print form, and for at least 20 years on the Internet. They provide a valuable and valued way of keeping in touch with a large audience. Of course sending a newsletter digitally decreases the costs, and shortens the time between sending and receiving, so you are able to be more topical.

You can send all your email newsletters directly from your computer, but as your numbers grow, it becomes harder work, and more time-consuming. In addition, you have to be there to send them. There are now many automated ezine services that will provide a range of useful features at low cost. These include list management, formatting, and several feedback statistics, such as the number of ezines that are opened (and hopefully read). My preferred ezine supplier is Constant Contact – **www.constantcontact.com** – which has never let me down in five years of continual use.

Ezines are a very effective way of keeping in touch with journalists, as well as current and prospective clients. If you make a commitment to produce an ezine, make sure that you deliver it regularly, whether it is weekly, fortnightly or monthly. Don't overdo the promotion, either. If your ezine is full of good tips, you will find that people ask if they can quote you.

I always say yes, provided they use this piece of text alongside it:

The information in this ezine may be freely re-used in any online or offline publication, provided it is accompanied by the following credit line - This information was written by Alan Stevens, and originally appeared in 'The MediaCoach', his free weekly ezine, available at www.mediacoach.co.uk

That ensures a publicity benefit to you wherever the information appears.

Never send spam (unsolicited email). You need to make sure that everyone who receives your ezine has opted-in to receive it. You should also make sure that it is easy to unsubscribe from your list, though if your content is good, no-one will want to.

30-Second Ezine Guide

✓ Publish regularly (weekly, monthly or quarterly)

✓ Never spam – make sure that everyone has opted in to receive it

✓ Don't make people go to your site to read the whole article

✓ Offer far more useful information than marketing material

✓ Write it yourself (even if it means publishing less often)

✓ Don't be afraid to be conversational. People like to get to know you

✓ Use humour. Making people smile is good!

✓ Encourage people to pass it on to their friends

✓ Occasionally, make special offers to subscribers

✓ Don't charge for it (and don't start it as a free service, then charge later)

✓ Mention other people, and other websites

✓ Encourage guest columnists

✓ Always write for your audience, never for yourself

Alan Stevens

Audio & Podcasting

The term Podcasting can be off-putting. It is simply the creation of an audio file that can be played through the speakers on a PC (or Apple Mac), or downloaded onto a MP3 player, such as an iPod (hence the name).

I don't have a podcast. I have a *Media Coach Radio Show*. Don't tell anyone, but it is exactly the same as a podcast, but calling it a radio show encourages more people to listen. However, since you aren't alarmed by calling it a podcast, I'll do that in this How-To guide.

Podcasting is a simple and effective way to deliver your message to people around the world. In essence, it is the creation of an audio file, which is then uploaded to a website. The file can be downloaded to PCs or portable MP3 players (often iPods, hence the name of the game). The real beauty of podcasting is that people can subscribe to your podcast, so that every time they plug their MP3 players into their PCs (a process known as synchronisation), they receive the latest version of your podcast.

In order to podcast, you need:

1. A PC with speakers and microphone

2. Sound recording software

3. A website to host the podcast

4. A way of promoting your podcast

The 4 Podcasting Essentials

Here's my advice for each of the elements.

1. A PC With Speakers And Microphone

Of course, you probably have one of these already, but I'd advice buying a headset with attached microphone. It's easier to use, and provides a better sound quality. The equipment simply plugs into the speaker and microphone sockets at the back of your PC. The cost is around 20 to 30 pounds, and is available from any computer store. If you pay a little more, you can get a switched version so that you don't have to unplug and replug if you want to use your PC speakers.

2. Sound Recording Software

There's lots of this around, and you can buy very sophisticated editing packages. I like to keep it simple, so I use Audacity, from **audacity.sourceforge.net** It is easy to use and free, so gets my vote. If you use it to create MP3 files (a good idea), then you need another piece of free software called the LAME Encoder. Both are available from the Sourceforge – **www.sourceforge.net** – website.

Simply download the software, and allow it to create an icon on your desktop. To create your podcast, click on the red button and start to speak. When you have finished, click on the yellow button. To save the file, click on File, then Export as MP3. Give the file a name, and include your name and the podcast title in the pop-up window. Save the file.

3. A Website To Host The Podcast

You can host the file on your own website, but this may require you to do some work. If you don't mind spending five dollars a month, you can use Libsyn.com. I've used them for a while now, and found them to be excellent. You simply create an account, log on, and upload your podcast file. You can provide other details, such as a brief description and a logo. A page will be created (you can select a template for the design), from which people can download your podcast. My page is at **mediacoach.libsyn.com**

4. Promoting Your Podcast

If you use a service like Libsyn.com, they will assist you to promote it to the major directories such as iTunes, iPodder and Podcast Pickle (honestly). In addition, you can search for podcast directories, and submit your podcast directly. The process is very simple. Finally, mention your podcast whenever you can, and provide links to it from your website(s). Encourage others to promote it too. Good luck.

30-Second Audio & Podcasting Guide

✓ Use a good-quality microphone

✓ Work from prompts, not a detailed script

✓ Include some theme music (available at very low cost from sites like stock20.com)

✓ Never use audio (such as music) without permission

✓ Carry a voice recorder with you at all times to capture interviews

✓ Publish audio regularly to build up a following

✓ Put your audio on iTunes

✓ Notify other podcast directories (your hosting service should help you do this) whenever you release a new show

Video & Vodcasting

I'm sure that you will know Youtube — **www.youtube.com** — the site where videos can be uploaded for free. However, you may not be aware that there are many people using Youtube for business promotion, by creating regular video programs (sometimes known as videoblogs, or vodcasts).

Take care if you decide to create internet video. It is as easy to do damage to your brand (probably easier) as it is to enhance it. The sight of a business owner doing a 10-minute piece to camera in an untidy office, with a script pinned up beside the camera, is not the image you should portray.

Good quality video cameras are cheap and widely available. I keep one handy at all times. You can use Windows Movie Maker (or its Mac equivalent) to edit and title your videos, and then upload them to Youtube. There is no need to use the highest quality, since the content is more important. Pay close attention to the sound, though, since that aspect can let you down badly.

Going Viral

Viral marketing is something that can be planned, but sometimes it just happens. For example, Judson Laipply became the most-watched man on the planet with his *Evolution of Dance* video – now with over 100 million viewings. I spoke to Judson last year in California, and he told me that he never intended the video to be seen by more than a handful of friends. However, he did one thing that made him a worldwide star, and ensured that he got plenty of calls – he put his contact details on the end of the video. So even if you aren't planning to go viral, make sure people can get in touch.

If you want to create a viral video, here's my best piece of advice – get lucky. Nobody seems to be able to predict what will catch the imagination of the web audience. You might produce 20 videos, but only one will go viral. I think it's like start-up companies. Nobody is ever sure which ones will survive. All things considered, I don't think I'd start a company that produces viral videos.

Nevertheless, there are some strategies that will give you a better chance of success with viral marketing. For one thing, you need a plan. You also need to be able to adapt quickly. Start slowly, and offer the video to influential bloggers and reviewers. Post it on Youtube, Facebook, Myspace and other similar sites. And don't worry if you fail. Just try again.

30-Second Video & Vodcasting Guide

- ✓ Keep the clips short – no more than seven or eight minutes
- ✓ Vary the content, using a voice-over at times to break it up
- ✓ Use establishing shots – a few seconds of a static image at the start
- ✓ Make sure that the audio quality is good
- ✓ Don't just become a talking head
- ✓ Use titles and credits
- ✓ Don't use effects at all – a simple cut from one scene to the next is fine
- ✓ Make sure that your contact details appear on every video
- ✓ Never, ever, upload video from TV (even if you are in it) without permission

Alan Stevens

Measurement & Analysis

All this advice will bring you in more business contacts, opportunities and real work. However, it would take a huge amount of effort to pursue every PR technique, leaving no time to fulfil your business obligations. In addition, you need to know which of your efforts was most successful in generating business, so that you can do more if it, or try to improve the effectiveness of other techniques.

You also need to know the cost-effectiveness of all your PR efforts, to determine whether your PR budget, however slim, is being well-spent. Not measuring and analysing your results means that much of your effort could be wasted.

So you need to measure the effectiveness of all your PR activities, and compare them with the targets set at the start of the campaign (you do set targets, don't you?). Fortunately, many of the techniques you have just read about are very easy to measure, especially those which make use of social media.

Traditional PR measures include:

Opportunities To See (OTS)

All possible viewings of a PR message by the target audience are added up. For example, a mention in a newspaper with a readership of one million would score one million OTS. Sometimes a monetary value will be attributed to the OTS, according to how much it would have cost to reach the same score by paid advertising.

Changes In Perception

By conducting awareness surveys before and after a PR campaign, it is possible to measure what impact the campaign had on awareness and brand image. However, this assumes that all other factors are neutral, and it may be that other events, such as bad news about the company or sector, could be a larger factor than PR.

Achieving A Specific Objective

This could be a change in the law, following a PR campaign by a pressure group.

Changes in sales volume. This is an easy thing to measure, but not always easy to attribute to PR.

Any of the above can be applied to PR campaigns in any medium. However, there are some measurement techniques that are specific to digital PR, such as:

Google Analytics

This is a tool that is free and simple to use, which provides a mass of detailed results. You should have this running on your site anyway, but it comes into its own when you are measuring how your site traffic changes. Among the measurements it delivers are:

- Number of unique visitors

- Sources of visitors

- Top performing keywords

- Length of time spent on site

- Entry point

- Exit point

- Whether a visitor takes up an offer (such as signing up for more information)

You should monitor your results regularly - probably daily during intense activity, but at least weekly. The results will allow you to refine your PR efforts in a classic feedback loop.

Twitter Followers & Facebook Fans

If you are trying to build a community of interest, then the simple increase in these numbers should be a useful guide.

Activity On Your Blog

The number and nature of comments left on your company blog will provide qualitative feedback about your PR efforts. Care is needed here, since there may be a few loud voices who are unrepresentative of your market as a whole. However, as a rule of thumb, it is often estimated that there are a hundred readers for each person who posts a comment (though don't use that statistic in your reports to the board). You can also encourage people to subscribe to your blog postings, and forward them on to others.

Mentions On Social Media Sites

You can also monitor the number of times your site is mentioned on various sites, using a range of alert services. For example, Twilert.com will send you an email each time a phrase or word that you specify is mentioned in a Tweet. Google Alerts is a more wide-ranging service that performs a similar function across the web.

More Sophisticated Techniques

There are a number of services that will offer you even more detailed analysis of the impact of your PR campaigns. Technorati.com (free) evaluates and ranks blogs in terms of their influence. Trucast and Trureputation from visibletechnogies.com, are paid-for services which analyse whether mentions of your organisation are positive or negative. Omniture.com is a chargeable service with extremely detailed analyses of your web messages (including pictures and video), wherever they appear.

As the old saying goes, "If you can't measure it, you can't manage it."

Unlike some old sayings, it happens to be true for PR, as it is for many things. It is neither difficult nor expensive to measure the impact of your PR campaigns. You should plan how you will measure at the same time as you plan everything else. Don't leave it to chance. In fact, you should take your first measurements before the campaign has started, otherwise how will you know if it worked?

Alan Stevens

Get Pinging

OK, you now know the essentials, you've got something to promote, and you are keen to get going. What should you do? Well (as usual) it depends on what you want to achieve. You may be launching a new product, reviving a tired brand, or indulging in a bit of self-promotion.

Here's a quick checklist to get your campaign started:

- ☐ Define your objective(s). Keep them simple
- ☐ Decide how your objectives will be measured
- ☐ Decide on the message you want to send out
- ☐ Decide on your target market
- ☐ Set up your measurement tools
- ☐ Conduct any pre-campaign surveys
- ☐ Decide what tools you will use
- ☐ If using social media, set up accounts if you don't already have them
- ☐ Decide whether to do it all yourself or use an agency
- ☐ Run final sanity checks to make sure that there is a potential return on investment
- ☐ Launch the campaign
- ☐ Monitor the results
- ☐ Amend the campaign if necessary
- ☐ At the end of the campaign, gather all the results together
- ☐ Analyse the results in detail
- ☐ Review your next PR activity

Simple, eh? In practice, any of these steps could entail substantial input of time and money. Sometimes, it is difficult to measure the bottom-line impact of PR campaigns. You need to try to quantify everything in order to justify your efforts, however. Whether you are promoting a small business or a huge corporation, the same principles apply. If you miss out any of the tasks above, you could waste your efforts.

Good luck!

Case Studies

A lot of companies are jumping on the social media bandwagon. Alas, many of them have failed to understand how to use traditional media, and their efforts, in any medium, are doomed to failure. The basic principles remain the same, whatever method you choose; the right message, at the right time, to the right audience. It really is that simple.

On the following pages are some examples of companies who really understand how PR works. Some are huge corporations, some tiny businesses. What they share is a commitment to engage with their customers, and respond to their messages. They don't subscribe to the maxim that the customer is always right, because in some cases, the customer isn't. However, customers of these companies feel that their concerns have been listened to and responded to. That's what's important.

These case studies are not by any means the only examples of integrated PR around. Nor are they necessarily the most effective. What they share is an understanding of how traditional and social media can be used together to deliver a simple, single message (now where did I read that before).

I'd like to thank all of the companies who gave their information freely, and were kind enough to agree to have their studies included in this book. I'm really grateful as I hope you will be after you have read them.

Alan Stevens

Dell Computers (Dell Outlet)

This first example is interesting, since it focuses particularly on one platform; Twitter. However, I have included it, since it shows how sales can be made, using the same message as offline, but with a social media twist.

Dell Outlet collects the equipment that is returned to Dell, so their stock levels can fluctuate quite a lot. When there is a large bubble of a particular model, there may be time to generate an e-mail campaign to promote that particular system and generate more demand. However, when the bubble is smaller, the main tactic to drive sales has been to lower the price of the overstocked model. The challenge for Dell Outlet was to figure out a way to generate more traffic and greater demand for their products.

Dell Outlet came up with the idea that Twitter could be a solution to the challenges presented, by offering Twitter-specific promotions and featured products. They set themselves three goals:

1. **To drive increased traffic**, and thus increased demand for particular products for which Dell Outlet had a large volume of stock.

2. **To grow the number of Dell Outlet's Twitter followers** to the point where it is sizable enough to have an impact on sales, by posting special offers.

3. **To increase the visibility of Dell Outlet** within the community of Twitter users and hence increase the likelihood of Twitter users to consider Dell Outlet for their next technology purchase.

By connecting with this group of potential customers that are likely to influence others who are not as technical or connected to social media, there could be a possibility of also influencing others beyond Twitter, since word of mouth is a very powerful strategy. Dell Outlet's Twitter strategy revolves around regularly posting special Twitter-only offers or highlighting great deals currently available on **www.twitter.com/delloutlet**. Launched in early June 2008, Dell Outlet currently has around three quarters of a million individual subscribers (followers) and hopes to continue to expand that base. When a new Tweet is posted, it generally directs followers to their Dell Outlet landing page for Twitter at **www.delloutlet.com/twitter**. There the Twitter-only promotion will appear only for the time period during which the offer is valid – typically until midnight that evening. After that point, visitors are invited to become followers of Dell Outlet on Twitter.

Furthermore, on Dell Outlet's Home and Home Office customer homepage, they have featured a similar invitation to subscribe to their Twitter postings at **www.delloutlet.com/home**.

Ricardo Guerrero led the development of strategy for Dell Outlet to use Twitter as a marketing vehicle and set up all the web pages and Twitter presence, while his colleague Stefanie Nelson has been responsible for maintaining those pages and creating the actual Tweets, with an attempt to post at least once every other week.

Dell Outlet's Twitter has linked to Dell's *Direct2Dell blog*, which is also posting its headlines on Twitter, and is currently in discussions to develop a strategy with other teams within Dell to create a unified Twitter presence.

Dell Outlet tracks the growth of followers as well as daily traffic metrics to the **www.delloutlet.com/twitter** *page*. Specifically, by tracking traffic to this page on the days that offers were posted to Twitter, a rough response rate to each posting can be calculated. Further, the actual use of each coupon code can also be tracked. The Twitter campaign is very successful, and Dell Outlet will continue to use this form of promotion in the future. They are frequently cites as one of the great Twitter success stories, having made millions of dollars worth of sales since the campaign began.

Alan Stevens

First Direct

First Direct (or as they style themselves, *first direct*) is a telephone and online bank in the UK, being a division of HSBC. They have no branches, and are based in Leeds, where I went to meet their Head of PR, Amanda Brown. They also happen to be my personal bank, so it was interesting, after 10 years of banking with them, to finally see the face of someone who works there.

They have been in business for over 20 years, and were launched with a quirky PR and advertising campaign around the slogan 'black and white banking'. They have retained the same style ever since, but have only recently experimented with social media. Their campaign came to my attention when I noticed that they were following me on Twitter. Somewhat alarmed to be stalked by a financial institution, especially my bank, I sent them a direct message which led to an interview with Amanda.

It turned out that I was not alone in my reaction, since one of the first responses to their campaign was a Tweet saying, "I'm not sure I want to be followed by a bank."

Amanda sees social media as getting back to the roots of public relations. "It's about talking to your customers through a medium. Social media is actually going to be really important in public relations terms but it is trying to understand what is relevant to us and what is not," she says.

In collaboration with the social media specialist public relations consultancy Wolfstar, the bank has now set up a social media newsroom – **www.newsroom.firstdirect.com** – to provide a service for professional PR people, bloggers and Tweeters.

"For example," said Amanda, "Increasingly, people are turning to online methods of media consumption and as a brand we have to go where the audience is. With the social media newsroom we wanted to create one central hub for all our communications online and we wanted to make those communications as portable and shareable online as possible. We create a lot of content that could add value to the conversations already going on online. The newsroom is a step on the way to engaging in that dialogue. A lot goes on at *first direct* which would not necessarily be newsworthy but says a lot about the business. It allows me to say someone has been sitting in a phone box all day to raise £3,000 for Childline. It gives people more insight into how we operate."

Interestingly, *first direct* has retained their core message and their brand image for their foray into social media. I think this is significant, since some brands seem to think that everything must change for the new audience on Twitter and Facebook. As it turns out, most of the audience is exactly the same, whatever medium is used. *first direct* understands that.

Shaquille O'Neal/Phoenix Suns

One of the greatest examples of bringing the power of social media into the world of PR has been the promotion of the Phoenix Suns basketball team, and their star player, Shaquille O'Neal, during his time there. The person responsible is Phoenix-based PR expert, Amy Martin — **www.twitter.com/digitalroyalty**.

Amy now helps to manage Shaquille's online presence, using a range of sophisticated measurement tools. Due largely to Amy's efforts, Shaquille has close to two million Twitter followers (**www.twitter.com/the_real_shaq**) and is regularly mentioned in the traditional press as an example of how to use social media well (creating yet more buzz). So how does it all work? I spoke to Amy on several occasions to find out.

A crucial factor is the speed and detail of monitoring the response to Tweets and updates on various sites. Amy has refined the functions of measurement software to allow her to see the effect of a single message. She calls it *Return on Influence* (a new form of ROI), which is distilled down to an index, showing whether the efforts have had a positive or negative impact on the brand, as well as by how much.

Amy has developed a Twitter strategy called *Random Act Of Shaqness*, which includes:

- Identifying influential fans and websites.
- Helping Shaquille create individual Tweets.
- Capturing events using audio, video and photos.
- Sending out messages and links to influencers.

Every single activity is tracked and measured, up to and including click-throughs to Shaquille's website, and whether a purchase is made online. Amy refers to the whole system as an *online ecosystem*, in which she can detect hotspots of key influencers or groups of fans, who can be targeted in later efforts.

The Phoenix Suns have also benefited as a whole from using social media. They have over 25 employees using Twitter, and each of them chats to fans (and future fans) on a personal level. They were probably the first sports organisation (or possibly the first organisation of any type) to digitally reveal the faces and personalities behind their logo. On their first Twitter night, in January 2009, the Suns were featured on over 300 websites, ESPN TV, and were mentioned thousands of times in Tweets. The exposure gained, relative to the effort put in (inviting fans in to meet the players) was huge. Not only that, but the positive mentions of the brand (analysed by the software mentioned above), soared, culminating in a large article about the event in *The New York Times*.

This case study is somewhat different from the others in this book, in terms of the precise monitoring used. I'm sure that it will set the standard for thousands of organisations to use social and traditional media to promote their brand. I predict we'll be hearing a lot more of Amy Martin, and whoever she works with.

The Scuderi Group

The Scuderi Group is not the sort of company that you might think would get involved in social media. They are, basically, engineers. To be precise, they are an engine development company of fluid and thermodynamic experts focused on improving the performance of the internal combustion engine.

As a start-up with a revolutionary new approach to the design of the combustion engine, The Scuderi Group faced a communications challenge. The company needed to convince key influencers in the automotive market that an engineering design that had not fundamentally changed in over a century could be radically altered in a way that would dramatically improve fuel efficiency while sharply cutting harmful emissions. The company needed to raise awareness, understanding, and acceptance of the revolutionary Scuderi Air-Hybrid Engine technology among a sceptical audience of automotive industry influencers and potential investors in a crowded and difficult market.

The Scuderi Group asked Topaz Partners **www.topazpartners.com**, a PR firm, to help them address the challenge. A guiding philosophy at Topaz Partners is that Web 2.0 and traditional media outreach are not mutually exclusive when it comes to public relations. These are the sort of guys who probably could have written this book. The goal in this campaign was to use social media tools and resources to gain wider visibility among traditional automotive and engineering media outlets for the Scuderi Group. Traditional media outlets, in turn, would help to promote their Web 2.0 initiatives, creating a kind of PR virtuous circle that would generate significantly more visibility together than as separate initiatives.

The solution to this tricky communications challenge consisted of two elements: information and distribution.

Information: the Scuderi Group enlisted the services of one of the world's top engineering research firms, Southwest Research, to study the engine design and to generate technical data about the engine that would be of particular interest to engineers. The Scuderi Group worked with Sonalyst Inc. to produce a top quality, highly informative series of videos about the engine's theory of operation and design. The Scuderi Group's president, Sal Scuderi, is an engineer by training, with an exceptional ability to speak about the Scuderi Air-Hybrid technology in clear terms both to engineering professionals, automotive reporters, and laymen. He's a perfect media spokesman (somewhat unusual in an engineer, and I speak as the son of one).

Distribution: Topaz Partners used Web 2.0 tools and resources to distribute the company's information and message across a targeted audience at low cost. A blog was launched – **www.scuderigroup.com/blog** – to promote Scuderi Group news and events, as well as related automotive and environmental news and is updated on a regular basis. Audio interviews with Scuderi executives are produced as podcasts on a regular basis.

Scuderi focused on newsy topics as well as design issues, and distributed them via the blog. Monthly e-mails were sent to a list of over 1,000 key automotive industry influencers and journalists, which included the latest company news and links back to the blog (you can see a trend here).

Sonalyst-produced videos were posted to YouTube, and distributed via Scuderi's dedicated YouTube Channel — **www.youtube.com/scuderigroup**. Videos were also promoted through company blog and e-mails. Media releases were sent to key automotive and engineering reporters, distributed over wire services, and posted on the blog. Reporters and editors were contacted about the Scuderi Group as news and editorial opportunities warranted. In short, the blog was the hub, and the spokes of the wheel were both social and traditional PR efforts.

Topaz Partners' integrated approach to public relations, using both mainstream and social media tools and resources, created the virtuous circle that they intended.

The blog quickly generated more than 70,000 page views; the Scuderi Podcast generates over 50 downloads a day. Views of the company's Theory of Operation video on YouTube have surged to over 100,000, and continue to increase. Scuderi YouTube videos are embedded into mainstream media online stories, increasing views and visibility. The Scuderi Group has received coverage in Wired News, Forbes, and Motor Trend, among others. Scuderi news stories and company videos are posted on social bookmarking websites, including Digg and Techcrunch, generating further visibility. Subscriptions to the Scuderi newsletter are in the thousands.

Topaz Partners concluded: "When it comes to social media and public relations, the sum is greater than the individual parts. Social media (including podcasts, blogs and videos) and traditional PR efforts are most effective and most powerful when used together as part of a coordinated strategy."

I couldn't have put it better myself.

Ford Motor Company

Ford knows a lot about how to sell cars, though in recent times they have been suffering, along with the rest of the motor trade. Huge corporations like Ford tend not to be at the forefront of PR innovation, and the idea of using social media to promote their products probably led to an interesting internal debate. However, they made the bold move to appoint a Head of Social Media, Scott Monty, with whom I've had conversations about a fascinating campaign.

He has a pragmatic view of social media:

"Let's not kid ourselves. Using social media as part of your marketing mix is far more than recruiting some über-connected individual who can bring attention to your brand. It starts with crafting a strategy and understanding what your business objectives are. And it means never, ever taking your eye off the customer and doing what matters - providing value to them. After all, isn't that what you're in business for?"

Exactly. So what was that fascinating campaign I mentioned? It's called the *Ford Fiesta Movement*, and is the campaign to introduce the Ford Fiesta into the USA. Personally, it's not the first car I'd think of advertising, but we've had it in the UK a lot longer, and is has developed a social mythology that is probably hard to shift. Ford decided to import a hundred Fiestas, and give them to drivers for six months for free, provided that they documented their experiences via Twitter, Facebook, YouTube and other social media sites. Over 4,000 people applied, and the process of selection became a media story in itself.

Everything is documented on a single website, **www.fiestamovement.com**, including photos, videos, Tweets and blogs. The drivers are known as *agents*, and their exploits can be followed individually online. Agents are given monthly *missions* based around a theme (for example style and design), and their reports are shared on the website. Some of the missions have been quite bizarre, for example, asking the agent to recreate Paul Revere's midnight ride by driving the historic route while discussing that part of American history and the difference between the drive in their car versus on a horse. Another mission is to turn their Fiesta into an ice cream truck. After stocking it with ice cream, they drive to the beach or an event and give away every piece, photographing each person who receives an ice cream. For the most adventurous, one mission is to get married in Las Vegas, in the most bizarre chapel they can find, in front of 10 witnesses. Not every mission is completed successfully, I might add, but that's part of the fun.

Scott Monty commented that the people in this programme are allowed to say whatever they want whenever they want.

"If you think − for one second − that Ford is telling these people what to say or that we're only looking for glowing reviews, I want some of what you're smoking." (That's just a figure of speech, of course.)

He also conceded that the campaign is a PR event, and not just an experiment in social media. Ford have had acres of print coverage, and plenty of TV and radio interviews, whenever one of the Fiestas rolls into a town.

As I write this, the campaign is still under way, so full evaluation is impossible. However, it seems to me that the payback for Ford, for the cost of 100 small cars, has already been enormous. It remains to be seen whether this is a model for marketing and PR in the future, or just a one-off brilliant stunt.

Alan Stevens

Tillamook County Creamery Association

Companies of any size can use integrated PR. Sometimes it's the smaller, more nimble ones who use it best. Tillamook County Creamery Association (TCCA) is a great example – **www.tillamookcheese.com**. In Spring 2008 the nearly 100-year-old company freed a small budget to fund one of its agency's big ideas. Tillamook enjoys strong brand awareness and sales in its core markets in the Northwest USA, but wanted to expand to other regions.

They engaged an agency, Conkling Fiskum & McCormick (CFM) – **www.cfm-online.com** – to help them. CFM believed that the best way to grow was through positive word-of-mouth from existing customers. A social networking strategy was developed to accelerate existing online conversations among those that loved the brand and take the company into its second century.

Allison McCormick, Principal at CFM, says, "It's harder and harder to reach the people you need to reach through traditional media. Last year, when we were planning the 100th anniversary campaign, we decided we should carve some time, and some budget, to move where the consumers are. And they're online."

In a Web 2.0 world, brands are in the hands of their customers. People would rather hear from each other than from companies. Fortunately for Tillamook, there have been Tillamook Cheese fans as long as there has been Tillamook cheese. They had begun sharing their affection for the brand on the Web, but not in a single location. Of course, the current social networking tools now allow those who share a common passion to come together. By early 2008, 400 Facebook members had joined fan-started Tillamook Cheese groups.

While consumers trust other consumers most, they also want to be listened to by the companies they are talking to or about. CFM wanted to engage Tillamook's best customers to deepen the connection they had with the brand to encourage them to pass on the message, so they decided to create a Tillamook fan community. They listed several advantages:

Providing Access To Inexpensive Research
Direct contact with customers would provide answers to questions Tillamook never thought to ask. By putting a priority on listening to its best customers, the company could profit from their insights. Through open and honest feedback from those who feel a personal connection to the brand, Tillamook could learn how best to invest its money – testing ads, generating new ideas for packaging design and new products, and identifying how best to connect with consumers.

Offering Constant Engagement With Consumers
Whether coming into contact with a consumer at Tillamook-sponsored event or at the supermarket, Tillamook could increase the brand's reach to customers on a consistent basis in a more cost-effective way than traditional advertising.

Allowing For Better Targeting Of Event
& New Product Promotions

They became able to invite fans in each market to nearby events and let them know when new products hit shelves in local stores.

Building A Group Of Tillamook Loyalists

Their brand advocacy could promote Tillamook products with high credibility and modest cost to everyone they know.

Measuring The Success Of Online
Investments In Real Time

The overall goal was to build a community around the Tillamook brand that would allow its most loyal customers to know it better, expand their relationship with the company, provide open and honest feedback, and spread the word about the brand to boost sales. Building a fan club has the advantage of being measurable on several levels. Because it is a database of self-selected Tillamook brand fans, its size, rate of growth and response to online initiatives could be benchmarked and measured very easily.

Because TMC is a century-old, farmer-owned co-op, CFM decided to take small, careful steps in developing the social networking strategy as a part of the company's public relations activity. CFM immediately began drafting a look for the Fan Club and a layout for the Web site meeting weekly with the client to ensure they felt ownership of the project.

Each new draft and revision was shared with the client and a clear timeline with detailed steps was drawn up to bring the client along comfortably. It's important to remember that lots of companies (maybe including yours) are nervous of social media. Some even get frightened by the idea of being on radio, come to think of it.

Facebook, Blogger and Twitter all played a part in the strategy, reinforcing the company's 100-year-old message. The Fan Club on Facebook was used initially as the hub of the online community. To encourage bloggers to continue or begin writing positive posts, favourite posts were highlighted and commented on, as well as being posted to the company's main website. In monitoring of online conversations, Tweets declaring love for Tillamook products were spotted. So a Twitter feed was featured prominently on the official Web site.

CFM then created **www.tillamookfanclub.com**.

The first phase of the site highlighted *Fans of the Month* who won a year's supply of cheese and other prizes for outstanding declarations of love for the brand. Tillamook personalities were profiled to show tradition and the real people within the company. Also included were popular recipes because, research showed interest in cooking was an influential component for the target audience. There was a product of the month that connected to the new online store and pushed sales. Most importantly, the site became a place for fans to share their story about their love for Tillamook using the *share with a friend* tool.

Were the customers ready for it? Yes. They were already talking and connecting online. The challenge faced by CFM was convincing a traditional company to launch into a new century by expanding the way it related to its customers. In order to make the farmer-owned co-op comfortable with making an online community the platform for its public relations strategy, they sold the benefits of access to free research, better marketing of events, and measurable outcomes.

Harold Strunk the CEO was so thrilled with what he saw he doubled the budget for Phase Two.

The final challenge was to convince fans to join.

The company didn't want them to do so solely for the possibility of winning prizes so CFM set about building a site that included what they knew they'd want to view and excite them enough to not only send in their stories, but encourage their friends to join.

A full-time in-house Online Community Manager was appointed to monitor and respond to the online community daily. Social media is a person-to-person communication system, so it's very important to have a face that people can talk to.

Heidi Luquette, the corporate communications manager at TCCA in Tillamook, sees social networking as more than a cheese-spreading tool. It's like a comment card that a visitor might fill out in the TCCA Visitor's Center, but even more accessible.

"I see it as an opportunity to learn more about Tillamook fans. Every day, it seems, we get an email from someone sharing a Tillamook story. Up until now, those stories have been hard to capture unless they're right here in front of us," Luquette said. "People tell us the good and the bad, and the memories they have. I think I understand more what people are saying, because they now have a new venue to say it."

I'll leave the last word on this case study to Tillamook County Creamery Association CEO, Harold Strunk:

"I have always been a strong supporter of communicating directly with our consumers. Social media tools are an important part of our communications strategy because they offer an effective way to engage with Tillamook loyalists as well as attract new consumers. Listening and being responsive to our consumer's needs has always been a core value for our company. Social media is a fantastic medium to gain a better understanding of what our consumers are thinking and saying about our brand. We believe interacting with people directly creates a much stronger emotional bond between the brand and consumers than any other form of communication. That emotional bond creates brand loyalty."

Pile of Sand

Pile of Sand Productions (POSP) – **www.pileofsand.com** – is an independent production company producing feature films, and is owned by Victor Imperi and Christopher Green. Doth Brands is a graphic design studio specialising in branding and identity. Doth most often works with small businesses and start-ups, and was engaged to work with POSP. To be honest, there is a family connection, since Cole Imperi is the owner of Doth Brands, and is also married to Victor Imperi, co-owner of Pile of Sand (that's nothing to do with what follows, but both they and I thought you ought to know).

Cole told me: "Social media levels the playing field. You have just as much pull with the masses as Puff Daddy or Starbucks. This is why social media can be great for business. Pile of Sand is different to most businesses. They depend on investors to fund their films. Once the film is funded and they produce it, it's time to sell it; hopefully at a sizeable profit to a distributor. Distributors base what they offer on several factors, but buzz among the public is certainly one of them. This is where social media comes in. Doth Brands wanted Pile of Sand to integrate social media fully into their business in order to put the generation of buzz into their hands.

"Victor and Chris are able to go grab a coffee and update Twitter, to go see a movie and post a review on their blog, or to get demographic info about their fans on Facebook through a cell phone. Social media is immediate feedback at all times; while it can be overwhelming for people new to it, it is a massive, massive resource."

Excellent points.

To a slightly lesser extent, small companies can also use traditional media to promote themselves, but it's harder to look big.

Pile of Sand has two blogs. Victor maintains one of them, Chris the other. Victor's posts are often shorter and centre around the film industry, film technique and film analysis. After he posts, it automatically updates his Twitter status. Then, Facebook is updated with the Twitter status automatically. By just doing one thing, Victor reaches the subscribers to his blog, his Twitter followers and then his Facebook friends. This amounts to hundreds and hundreds of people.

Right now, with no film currently in production, Pile of Sand's diehard fans and people genuinely interested in the 'science' of film mostly read the blogs and chat with the guys on social networking pages.

Victor and Chris utilise Twitter to keep an eye on the competition, find actors and other talent, locate potential crew, chat with local business owners (that may or may not become locations) and to be themselves. They are unique in that they're film producers that are accessible. Once the film nears production, both blogs change into updates, including things like casting calls, photos of craft services, behind the scenes video clips...

All their social media efforts switch into buzz generating mode. Twitter will become a check on what's happening with the film via the owner's cell phones. The blogs house actor interviews, pictures and video. The Facebook fan page hosts giveaways of movie merchandise and announce extra calls. Finally, Doth Brands actively promotes POSP to PR and media professionals who will hopefully do a story or feature on them, bringing in more traditional media.

Pile of Sand expects to reduce their advertising/marketing budget by around 90 per cent. They only advertisements Pile of Sand is looking at running are announcements in local publications listing casting calls. Everything else is being done solely on social media. Victor Imperi made some great points, so I've recorded them in full here.

On Independent Film

"The independent film industry has grown tremendously even in just the last five to 10 years. The words 'independent film' used to make people cringe; bringing to mind 25-minute grainy black and white films starring someone's girlfriend with an audience of 10 people.

"Look at the Oscars in 2009 where three of the five films nominated for Best Picture were independent; *The Reader, Milk* and *Slumdog Millionaire*. And *Slumdog* won. If you go back over the past few years, this trend has been increasing. Look at *Juno* last year, *Little Miss Sunshine* before that. I think it kind of began around 2000 with *American Beauty*. Independent films have a much wider audience as they're situated in the market along studio pictures and people just can't tell a difference at this point."

On Social Media And Adding Buzz To The Film

"Buzz is important for any movie, but really it's especially important for independent films. Unless you can get a big studio behind you, one difference between independent films and studio films is that they don't have huge marketing budgets. So, we don't have a huge marketing budget and we need to use every avenue that we have at our disposal. We need to utilise anything that we have at our disposal. Social media is one of those things. For a large company and a small company, social media plays no favourites. If we utilise it correctly, we have a real shot at being much more successful than our larger competitors.

"We're willing to be the point of contact; the filmmakers are the ones willing to be the one's putting the information out there. We're taking away that wall and that makes us so much more appealing and interesting to the average consumer.

"Plus, this allows us to start growing our fan base two years before the film will hit the market. This helps us start gaining a following now, when we're still in pre-production. But, by talking about it on these social networks, by the time it gets to the festivals, we've already got an audience talking and buzzing about the film. With Independent Film, the audience doesn't need to be huge or massive from the get-go. It needs a localized fan base that spreads, that ripples out.

"The pitfall with this is that this is a long time to engage the audience over a long period of time. But, if you use it correctly, it's a great way to exponentially expand your audience without spending any money and they're already there as soon as the film comes out as opposed to waiting until after the movie comes out to try to begin building buzz. We're banking on the fact that this gives our films more buzz that the other films coming out around the same time."

On Initial Reactions To Doth Brands Proposing Social Media

"Being a pretty private person myself, I was not at first thrilled at the thought of documenting my day-to-day thoughts and activities and routines. It wasn't that I didn't necessarily believe in the power of social media; I just wasn't a person that naturally did it before. I knew that there were people and companies that used it exceptionally well; I didn't know that I could. A big hurdle for anyone when they get started with social media is 'what do I say'. You've got this big forum and I don't want to waste it but how am I going to tie this in to me as a business and how am I going to make this interesting? That is a lot to digest at first. And, on top of that, you've got hundreds of possible different outlets for this. How do you choose which ones to use and really, you're not just choosing one, you're still choosing five, maybe 10. And how do I keep all of those up to date when I've got so many other things that I've got to keep organised? How do I integrate this into my life?

"I definitely knew that it was a good idea and I knew that it was the right way to go, and we certainly had enough evidence presented, it was just getting over my own initial anxiety of the prospect of it. My partner, Chris, is - to a certain extent - a bit more of a natural at it. I will say that each of our roles in our social media marketing sphere is tailored to us as individuals. I try to do more day-to-day and week-to-week, and Chris is able to sit down and write a more extensive post on some nuance of *Wake Up!* Or on some other film or even film history. When first proposed, Chris's initial reaction was, 'Give me a blog and I'll go crazy, you might be opening the floodgates'. He was ready to pour all of his ideas out to the world."

On Overall Experience With Social Media

"Getting involved with social media has been great for us. It's had, especially for me, some unintended effects. It's definitely daunting at first, but it causes you to focus on your business and define it, and to develop the personality of your business. People don't think about that. By thinking about how you're going to present yourself to the world on a day-to-day basis, you naturally develop a voice to your business and a personality and a place. Had we not done this, I think eventually we wouldn't have gotten there, but it would have taken us longer and it would have been more risky. We've got to develop our voice and our place while being relatively unknown at the first. We're not figuring this out in the face of investors; it has focused us and made us better able to talk about Pile of Sand and to explain who we are and what we do. Social Media has eliminated a lot of risk for us.

"I think that undoubtedly, social media can be beneficial to any business when used correctly. It can be wasted though, and I can say there have been times when I've flirted with wasting it. I think for small businesses especially competing with bigger, well-established businesses, I think it should be an unavoidable thing, like taxes. It is completely necessary. It is the only place where you'll be totally level with someone else and the only place where you can have a potential advantage against your larger competitors with more money and resources.

"People want to connect with people.

"I think if you look at the corporations who use it the best, they're using it as a person and not as a company, for example Ford and Starbucks. Starbucks on Twitter is still Starbucks, but it's a person you can talk to. As relates to our investors, it relates in a large way the same way to our audience. If investors can see that we're already gathering a following, they feel more secure. When we start going more heavily into production, it's a great way to keep our investors up to date and involved without adding meetings and sending reports. Investors either want to know as much as they possibly can or they don't want to know anything.

"Social media will answer any question they have and they can instantly see what is going on. It allows an individual to form a personal relationship with your company. There is some connection there that seems to be very innate to humans; they want connections.

"That's why we call all these people 'friends' online; these people we don't know or see. Social media has made us a safer bet. If nothing else, it shows the people that are entrusting you with their money that you are using every opportunity available to you .If I saw someone not using this, I would want to know what reasons they have for wasting that opportunity. Especially for someone in the entertainment industry. That's what all of this is, and for someone in that industry to waste that chance is inexcusable."

It's clear that this small film company has understood the power of social media, while not forgetting how valuable traditional PR still is. Good luck to them, and the many other companies now coming to the same realisation.

What's Next?

It's always tough to make predictions. No, I take that back. It's easy to make predictions. The tough thing is to make predictions that turn out to be true. Even in the short time between writing this book, and it appearing in your artistic fingers, new ways of delivering a PR message will have appeared.

It's apparent that both audio and video, though hardly new technologies, are having an increasing impact on the business of PR. Some companies, such as ASDA in the UK, have already made use of YouTube to run successful campaigns and reach a market incredibly fast. User-generated content (the stuff that you and I produce and upload) is becoming more acceptable and widespread than simple text comments on blogs and social networks. Sites like **www.12seconds.tv** and **www.audioboo.com** are becoming popular for uploading short video and audio clips.

There are a number of trends that are affecting all of the PR channels discussed in this book:

Increased Transparency

It will be much harder for companies to hide things, or deny that events have occurred, since the ability of all of us to capture and transmit information will continue to grow.

Increased Coverage

As the viral phenomenon has shown, it is possible for information to travel to every part of the world within seconds. It is not easy to predict what will go viral, so it may not be a particularly useful PR tool, but capitalising on the viral effect certainly will be an increasingly important PR function

Increased Knowledge

Consumers of products and services will be much more informed (and sometimes misinformed) about them. This presents a challenge to PR practitioners, but it is something that I, for one, welcome.

Increased Expectations

Clients of PR agencies will have a greater understanding of the tools used, because they also use them. There will be a need for agencies to demonstrate significant added value.

Increased Exchange of Information

As mentioned above, and throughout this book, there will be a huge demand from consumers to engage in dialogue with companies. Some already do it very well, by identifying individuals to run their Twitter accounts or Facebook groups. Of course, *plus ça change, plus c'est la même chose*, and the art and science of PR will continue much as before. As mentioned at the very start of this volume, we'll have new tools.

Resources & Links

For more information about the use of tools mentioned in this book, visit **www.mediacoach.co.uk/resources.htm**, where you will find advice, links and tools to help you in your PR efforts.

You can also subscribe to my free weekly email newsletter full of PR advice, and find out how to listen to *The Media Coach Radio Show* and watch *The Media Coach TV Show.*

Useful Websites

Expert Sources: **www.expertsources.co.uk**
An essential place for UK-based experts to be found. Many journalists use this as a source of expertise.

Press Choice: **www.presschoice.com**
This is similar to Expert Sources, but aimed more at large corporate organisations who want to be heard on national news.

Find a TV Expert: **www.findatvexpert.com**
If you are looking to become an expert on a TV series, this is the place for you.

Blogger: **www.blogger.com**
The blogging service owned by Google which will provide you with a free site to blog away to your heart's content.

Twitter: **www.twitter.com**
The micro-blogging service.

Linkedin: www.linkedin.com
A business-oriented social network.

Facebook: www.facebook.com
A personal and business social network.

Ping: www.ping.fm (not to be confused with this book!)
A service which allows you to update your status on all your social networks at once.

Constant Contact: www.constantcontact.com
An excellent web-based email newsletter service

Sourceforge: www.sourceforge.net This is the site from which to download the free audio editor, Audacity.

Libsyn: www.libsyn.com
A hosting service for podcasts.

Itunes: www.itunes.com
Apple's audio and video download service

YouTube: www.youtube.com
A free video hosting service, with over a billion hits so far.

Google Analytics: www.google.com/analytics
An excellent free service to analyse your website traffic.

Google Alerts: www.google.com/alerts
An invaluable way to monitor what people are saying about you (and anything else) online.

Technorati: www.technorati.com
Blog evaluation software.

Visible Technologies: www.visibletechnologies.com
Suppliers of web analysis software Truereputation and Trucast.

12 Seconds TV: www.12seconds.tv
A site to upload videos no longer than…12 seconds!

AudioBoo: www.audioboo.com
A site for uploading audio files of up to five minutes, and is tailored specifically for iPhones.

Case Study Websites

Dell Outlet: **www.delloutlet.com/home**
Dell Outlet Twitter: **www.twitter.com/delloutlet**
Dell Outlet Twitter landing page: **www.delloutlet.com/twitter**
first direct: **www.firstdirect.com**
first direct social newsroom: **www.newsroom.firstdirect.com**
Amy Martin's Twitter: **www.twitter.com/digitalroyalty**
Shaquille O'Neal's Twitter: **www.twitter.com/the-real-shaq**
Topaz Partners: **www.topazpartners.com**
The Scuderi Group: **www.scuderigroup.com**
The Ford Fiesta movement: **www.fiestamovement.com**
Tillamook Cheese: **www.tillamookcheese.com**
Conkling Fiskum and McCormick: **www.cfm-online.com**
Tillamook Fan Club: **www.tillamookfanclub.com**
Pile of Sand Productions: **www.pileofsand.com**

Recommended Reading

The New Rules of Marketing and PR by David Meerman Scott, ISBN: 978-0470379288
A brilliant summary of how the PR rules are changing. David is a real expert with an easy communication style.

Twitter Power: How to Dominate Your Market One Tweet at a Time by Joel Comm, ISBN: 978-0470458426
A New York Times best-seller, and rightly so. I've worked with Joel, and he is undoubtedly one of the top Twitter experts in the world.

Facebook Marketing: Leverage Social Media to Grow Your Business by Steve Holzner, ISBN: 978-0789738028
The best book around for Facebook users to learn how to promote their business.

How to Really Use Linkedin: Discover the True Power of Linkedin and How to Leverage It for Your Business and Career by Jan Vermeiren, ISBN: 978-1439229637
I know Jan well, and I've seen him present his great ideas to audiences. I always seem to learn something new and valuable from browsing through this book.

Can We Do That?!: Outrageous PR Stunts That Work – And Why Your Company Needs Them by Peter Shankman, ISBN: 978-0470043929
The best book I've ever read on PR stunts, by New York's finest PR practitioner

This is Social Media: Tweet, Blog, Link and Post Your Way to Business Success by Guy Clapperton, ISBN: 978-1906465704
A terrific primer on social media skills from a man who walks his talk.

Don't Make Me Think!: A Common Sense Approach to Web Usability by Steve Krug, ISBN: 978-0321344755
The best (and most entertaining) book that I know on how to create a user-friendly web presence

**The Design of Everyday Things by Don Norman,
ISBN: 978-0465067107**

A book every designer (that includes you, if you have
a website) should read. It shows you how design
principles can make things easier, and therefore more
attractive to your customers.

**Know Me, Like Me, Follow Me: What Online Social
Networking Means for You and Your Business by
Penny Power, ISBN: 978-0755319510**

The co-founder of business social network Ecademy
shares her philosophy for social networking success.
Full of excellent advice.

**Purple Cow: Transform Your Business by Being
Remarkable by Seth Godin, ISBN: 978-0141016405**

All of Seth's books are useful, so read this one and
check out the others too.

**What Clients Love by Harry Beckwith,
ISBN: 978-0446527552**

Great bite-sized chunks of advice from a real expert

**Managing the Message by Peter Hobday,
ISBN: 978-1902809182**

The low-down on how the media really works, from a
very experienced broadcaster.

**Drop Dead Brilliant by Lesley Everett,
ISBN: 978-0071494274**

The essential primer on personal branding, from one
of the world's leading experts.

Get Noticed: How To Boost Your Small Business Profile In 30 Days Or Less by Paula Gardner, ISBN: 978-0954568177

This book should be on every small company's bookshelf.

The 20 Best and Worst Questions Reporters Ask by David Avrin, ISBN: 978-0615266045

A brilliant book that will help you make the most of your media interviews.

Media Training A-Z: A Complete Guide To Controlling Your Image, Message, & Sound Bites by T J Walker, ISBN: 978-1932642360

America's top media trainer gives spot-on advice

Full Frontal PR by Richard Laermer, ISBN: 978-1576601811

How to refine your media message so that people will see you as a real expert

I See Your Name Everywhere by Pam Lontos, ISBN: 978-1600374807

Pam is one of the top PR experts in the US, and someone I often refer people to. This book is essential reading.

**Media Appearance Secrets by Clive Simpkins,
ISBN: 978-0620431125**
Clive is undoubtedly the top media expert in Southern Africa, and one of the best in the world. Great, readable advice.

**Guerrilla PR: Wired by Michael Levine,
ISBN: 978-0071382328**
The PR street-fighter on how to do PR online. Brilliant.

How to Be King of the Media Jungle by Chris Roycroft-Davis, ISBN: 978-0955723704
Former Executive Editor of The Sun newspaper with the inside track on how the media really works

**Brain Droppings by George Carlin,
ISBN: 978-0786891122**
In fact, any book by the late George Carlin is worth reading, since in my opinion he was not only the funniest man who ever lived, but he knew how to craft a message.

The Gorillas Want Bananas: The Lean Marketing Handbook for Small Expert Businesses by Debbie Jenkins & Joe Gregory, ISBN: 978-0954568108
First published in 2003 this book strikes out at the old wasteful marketing approaches and shows you how to get more success by spending less using PR, the internet, writing and networking. Ahead of its time.

10 Media, Social Media & Experts To Follow

1. Shawne Duperon: **www.twitter.com/shawnetv**
   Great advice for would be media stars.

2. Joel Comm: **www.twitter.com/joelcomm**
   US-based Twitter expert.

3. Mark Shaw: **www.twitter.com/markshaw**
   UK-based Twitter expert.

4. Peter Shankman: **www.twitter.com/skydiver**
   New York PR genius.

5. Guy Clapperton: **www.twitter.com/guyclapperton**
   A UK journalist with huge expertise.

6. Amy Martin: **www.twitter.com/digitalroyalty**
   The real expert on ROI (Return on Influence).

7. Scott Monty: **www.twitter.com/scottmonty**
   Ford's digital media guru.

8. Sarah Evans: **www.twitter.com/prsarahevans**
   One of the top PR experts around.

9. Guy Kawasaki: **www.twitter.com/guykawasaki**
   The man who knows all the good stories.

10. Robert Scoble: **www.twitter.com/scobleizer**
    The Silicon Valley blogger supreme.

About Alan Stevens

Alan Stevens is the Director of MediaCoach.co.uk, a company that provides communication skills to chief executives and company spokespeople.

He has been both a TV presenter and an expert interviewee on TV and radio shows worldwide. In the latter capacity, he has given over 2,000 radio and TV interviews, so is uniquely placed to give insights about the media, and how companies and individuals can improve their image.

He is a Member of the Chartered Institute of Public Relations, a Fellow of the Professional Speakers Association and also President-Elect of the Global Speakers Federation.

For over 25 years, he has appeared regularly on BBC TV News, Sky News, CNN, and Bloomberg, as well as on hundreds of radio stations.

He has been quoted in every UK newspaper, *The New York Times, Forbes Magazine, The Economist* and many others.

In 2006, The Independent newspaper listed him as: "One of the top 10 media experts in the UK."

His client list includes; Virgin, The Dorchester, Glaxo, The Savoy, Dubai Stock Exchange, North Yorkshire Police, EDF, Barclays, Sony Ericsson, Mumm Champagne, BP, Guinness World Records and BMW.

His popular book *The Pocket Media Coach* was published by HowToBooks in November 2005. He is also the co-author (with Jeremy Nicholas) of *MediaMasters*, also published by BookShaker.com.

Alan can be contacted:

- by Email: **alan@mediacoach.co.uk**
- on Twitter: **www.twitter.com/mediacoach**
- by Phone: **+44 20 8220 6919**

He welcomes feedback, which could lead to a mention for you in the next edition.

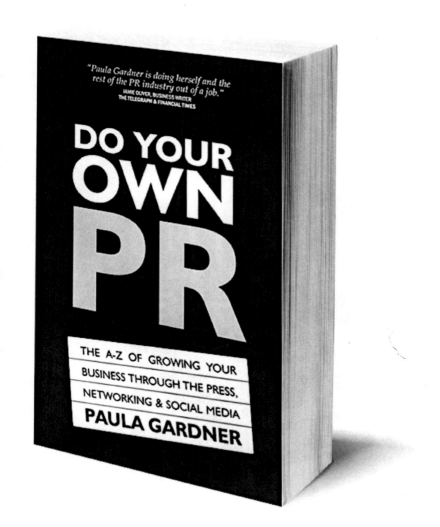

"An invaluable guide, full of insights."
Martin Kelner
THE GUARDIAN

MEDIA
Masters

Insider Secrets from the
big names of broadcast,
print and social media

Alan Stevens &
Jeremy Nicholas

www.publishingacademy.com

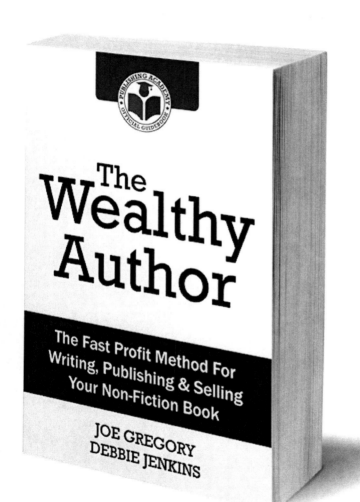

Lightning Source UK Ltd.
Milton Keynes UK
11 October 2010

161100UK00001B/11/P